Why You Can't Dispense Food Like Medicine

Praise For
Why You Can't Dispense Food Like Medicine

"This is a comprehensive playbook where employees at all levels are called upon to attentively and thoughtfully engage across their organization. Employees can create, deliver, and constantly improve a kind, respectful, empathetic community environment. Cindy's book helps them elevate the quality of life for all residents, directly contributing to measurable improved resident, family, staff, and corporate outcomes."

Paul Allison, Loving Family Caregiver

"Cindy's new book, *Why You Can't Dispense Food Like Medicine*, has opened my eyes to the vital role that hospitality plays in the mealtime service of members of senior care communities. It's not just the food that matters, the quality of the hospitality and service matters too!"

John L. Holahan, Inventor/President, SimplyThick, LLC

"If you work in senior living, Cindy Heilman's *Why You Can't Dispense Food Like Medicine* introduces new standards for hospitality and resident care, showing how kindness and respect can improve dining experiences, resident outcomes, and community census."

Carol Sapp, RD LD MBA, Chief Executive Officer, DiningRD

"Cindy Heilman makes the case that a hospitality framework in dining is central to supporting residents and staff in co-creating a strong and supportive community. Cindy's experience training staff to focus on hospitality is combined with her love for older adults and the staff who care for them. She draws from this experience to show how a commitment to hospitality at all levels in a community contributes to person-centered care and a nurturing work environment."

Diana White, PhD Institute on Aging Portland State University

"I have known Cindy for over 25 years and have had the privilege of observing her exceptional dedication to the senior living industry. The guidance that Cindy provides in *Why You Can't Dispense Food Like Medicine* would have greatly contributed to shaping the resident-centered dining experience I strove to achieve when I began my career in this field.

Her acclaimed Kind Dining program exemplifies a holistic philosophy by engaging the entire organization in meal service, extending far beyond the foodservice department. Her book details practical strategies for elevating the dining experience for residents, illustrating how these efforts positively influence families and the broader community. She wisely underscores that staff training should be viewed as an investment, citing significant benefits that far outweigh the costs."

Colleen A. Zenk, MS, CDM CFPP

"As a nursing home administrator you can't underestimate the power of learning, for yourself and for your team. To discover the value of creating a dining experience that contributes to residents' quality of life, administrators and other key leaders should read *Why You Can't Dispense Food Like Medicine.*

This book offers leaders the opportunity to learn why hiring people whose personal values align with professional motivations creates an unstoppable team of exceptional caregivers. Throughout this book Cindy offers advice on why and how to create this exceptional team.

If you value resident comfort, dignity, and well-being and want to create a foundation for meaningful relationships that enhance quality of life, begin by reading and sharing this book with your team."

Sarah McEvoy, Long-Term Care Chaplain, NHA, JD, Co-convener
Elder Care Research Network Transforming Chaplaincy

"In today's world where technology, inclusive of AI, is all the focus, Cindy steps in and reminds us of the importance of human connection. Single, personal moments to build relationships matter! As a 30+ year restaurant owner, I know first-hand guests judge the quality of the food and their overall dining experience with the quality of the service provided. In seniors housing, this perception of reality is magnified—and your residents won't hold back their thoughts and feelings. Incorporation of Cindy's 'how-to primer' will be a gamechanger for savvy, people-development operators as they serve the next generation of residents."

Nancy Swanger, PhD, Founding Director, Granger Cobb Institute for The Business of Aging, School of Hospitality Business Management, Carson College of Business

"As I was reading Cindy Heilman's new book, *Why You Can't Dispense Food Like Medicine*, I was reminded of something that I share with all my MHA students the first day of class. That is, healthcare management and leadership is a relationship-based business. Despite all our tools and technology, when distilled down to its essence, healthcare is fundamentally grounded in the many human moments that we encounter every day. This wonderful book expresses clearly how dining service in senior care organizations can be enhanced simply when people throughout the organization care for the needs of their residents and for one another. The lessons and techniques that Cindy talks about in this book are transferable to all service sector organizations. Her Kind Dining training has at its heart the realization that kindness displayed consistently and with purpose can be the deciding factor between a good healthcare organization and one that is truly great."

Leonard H. Friedman, **PhD, MPH, FACHE**, Professor and Director, MHA@GW Program, Department of Health Policy and Management, Milken Institute of Public Health, The George Washington

"The dining experience is the heart of any residential operation. Cindy played a key role in our signature success, and it is an honor to see her subsequent career in food service blossom over the years. Her raison d'etre is to inspire and create dining hospitality in residential communities. This book is a testament to her wisdom, experience, and philosophy—her words will resonate with readers."

Lisa Louie, Founding Program Director for False Island

"Cindy's book makes a compelling and evidence-informed case that food cannot be 'dispensed' in the same way as medication without losing its human meaning. Meals are moments of connection, identity, and belonging—particularly for older adults whose social worlds may be narrowing. The book's focus on training and workforce development is especially timely.

At a moment when senior care providers are grappling with staffing shortages, burnout, and turnover, *Why You Can't Dispense Food Like Medicine* reminds us that investing in people—particularly those who are often the lowest paid and least formally trained—yield returns in resident outcomes, staff engagement, and community reputation. The dining room becomes a living laboratory for culture change, where respect, consistency, and empathy can be practiced daily.

This book is an important contribution to the senior living and post-acute care literature. It should be required reading for anyone responsible for shaping resident experience, workforce culture, or quality outcomes in aging services."

Dr. Christian A. Mason, CALA, CNHA, FACHCA, DBA,
Senior Health Care Executive & Researcher,
Senior Services Research Collaborative (SSRCollab)

"This book nurtures the human spirit with an attitude of hospitality and civility. From teens to elders, all can benefit from how to transform the environment into a community. It is motivating, relevant and applicable beyond senior care communities."

Audrey Morgan, Career Long Term Care Foodservice Manager, NDTR, LDT

"When we dine with our seniors, we recreate a sense of community and, dare I say, a sense of family and fellowship. As leaders in senior caregiving environments, it is clear that staff may have widely varied experiences regarding meals and may require hospitality training. Among the many challenges in care environments, ensuring seniors consume adequate nutrients remains a priority. This is a much-needed book."

Dr. Pamela Straker, Author of *Heroic Caregiver*, Speaker, and Organizational Psychologist

Why You Can't Dispense Food Like Medicine

How Intentional Staff Relationships Shape Well-Being In Senior Living

Cindy Heilman, MS, NDTR, FAND

Creator of Kind Dining® Training

HEALTH AUTHORITY BOOKS

Why You Can't Dispense Food Like Medicine

How Intentional Staff Relationships Shape Well-Being In Senior Living

Printed in the United States of America.

ISBN 13: 978-1-966168-74-4
Library of Congress Control Number: 2026907290

Designed by Melissa Farr, Back Porch Creative, LLC

HEALTH AUTHORITY BOOKS
2511 WOODLANDS WAY
OCEANSIDE, CA 92054
www.healthauthoritybooks.com

Health Authority Books is an imprint of Indie Books International, Inc.

Dedication

This book is dedicated to all my clients who believe training is an investment in their employees. To all their employees who shared their enjoyment of and learning insights from their Kind Dining training experience, applied at work and at home. To those who continue to embrace the opportunity to grow personally and professionally for this noble cause of serving aging adults and one another around the dining table and beyond it.

Contents

Foreword

A couple of years ago I co-authored a book with Dan Collard called *Rewiring Leadership in Post-Acute Healthcare*. We wrote this book because the post-acute landscape has changed so much and so quickly that the old methods the industry has leaned on for years no longer work well, if at all. It's time to rethink the way we do certain things.

At the heart of this rewiring is good training and development. It's what builds leaders that can successfully navigate a tough (and often understaffed) environment and create a culture that makes good people want to stay. So, when Cindy Heilman asked me to write the foreword for *Why You Can't Dispense Food Like Medicine*, which also shines a spotlight on training and development in a very specific area, I was grateful to have the opportunity.

First, my own experiences in the post-acute arena have given me so much admiration for those who do this work. They care for people who are at a vulnerable stage of life. They have chosen this field even though it is hard. They care deeply. They want to serve and to make a difference.

We owe it to them, and of course to those they care for, to equip them with the tools and tactics to help.

Also, I love Cindy's Kind Dining concept. How we serve our patients and residents is a powerful subject that isn't explored nearly enough. Good food, well-prepared and served with respect and love, is one of the greatest human pleasures. It can bring up strong emotions and memories. It can provide comfort when we need it. This matters when we're well and it *especially* matters when we're in need of care.

Having worked in healthcare most of my life, I've noticed food is a huge part of the patient experience. Good food is good medicine. And preparing and serving it well is not just about food safety, quality, temperature, or even flavor (though all these matter). It's also about the friendliness of those who serve the food, the dignity with which they treat people, and the fellowship that happens around the table. People are hungry not just for food but for kindness, friendship, connection. In a real sense, mealtime is (or should be) a healing experience.

All of this is true in any care setting. Yet in a senior living community or post-acute facility, mealtime takes on even greater importance. It is often the highlight of a resident's day. It's when they can get out of their room and interact with others. It's when relationships are being formed with staff members and fellow residents. It's when people start to think "This is where I belong" . . . or (more concerning) when they don't.

In other words—and Cindy spells this truth out early in the book—mealtime is actually a powerful marketing event. What happens in the dining room, and the word-of-mouth that follows that, is a big factor in helping people decide whether to choose your community (or stay in it once they've chosen it). She then lays another truth on the reader: *You're dependent on your lowest-paid, least-trained staff to manage your most important experience.*

Her message is clear: Investing in your food service leaders and staff is a crucial business imperative. Make sure frontline employees are trained to do things like prepare a welcoming dining room, follow excellent service standards, get to know residents' favorite food (and alert them when it's on the menu), and help break the ice and get people talking. These may seem like simple things on the surface, but they really aren't. It is safe to say that most people don't naturally have this skill set. They need to be nurtured and developed.

The great news, as I've mentioned, is that the people who do this work already care (and that's more than half the battle). Their hearts are already in the right place. They want to make a difference in the lives of their patients. Otherwise, they would not have chosen this work. There are far easier jobs out there that don't require such a high emotional price.

In *The Calling: Why Healthcare Is So Special* I wrote that people enter healthcare because they have a deep longing to be helpful and useful. That calling lives just as strongly in the dining room as it does anywhere else. At times, its voice can get lost in the day-to-day stress and overwhelm. Cindy reminds us that when we train people well and honor their role, we help them find that voice again and unlock that compassion that brought them here in the first place.

If we can provide the sense of belonging these employees crave and the practical skills to do their job well—in a way that creates a great experience for residents—they will begin to find a deeper fulfillment in their work. When we have a place to go everyday where the work feeds our spirit, we want to keep coming back every day.

I also appreciate how practical this book is. Cindy doesn't just explain *why* Kind Dining matters, she shows us *how* to make it real. Leaders will come away knowing exactly what to reinforce, what to coach, and where to invest their time and energy. That kind of useful doable advice is what our people—and our residents—deserve.

Thank you, Cindy, for this needed reminder: When we invest in people and help them do their work well, we create places where residents feel they belong and employees rediscover just how much their work matters.

Quint Studer
Author of *The Calling: Why Healthcare is So Special*
Co-author of *Rewiring Leadership in Post-Acute Healthcare: Equipping Leaders to Succeed*

Preface

I believe every staff member can positively impact residents' nutritional health and well-being, as well as the organization's financial success, through a Kind Dining experience.

And to quote author Quint Studer, from his book, *Rewiring Leadership in Post-Acute Healthcare*,[1] "It is always a good time to reconnect experience to clinical outcomes."

Many say this is too complex. This is not my experience in the dining environment. Either you know the value of setting the table correctly or you don't. Either you know the value of offering a second cup of coffee or you don't. Either you know the value of serving ketchup with french fries or you don't. And you either come to the table with a positive attitude, or you don't.

Hospitality is a vital ingredient at every meal because it demonstrates we care about you. We all want a sense of belonging, and we have lost some of the humanity that makes including others a natural part of being in a senior living and post-acute care community—or any community, for that matter.

There is science and psychology behind this movement. Research from Press Ganey[2] and others[3] shows that if residents are happy dining in your community, they are more satisfied with living there. When they eat with other residents more often, they have a higher reported level of satisfaction with their lives.

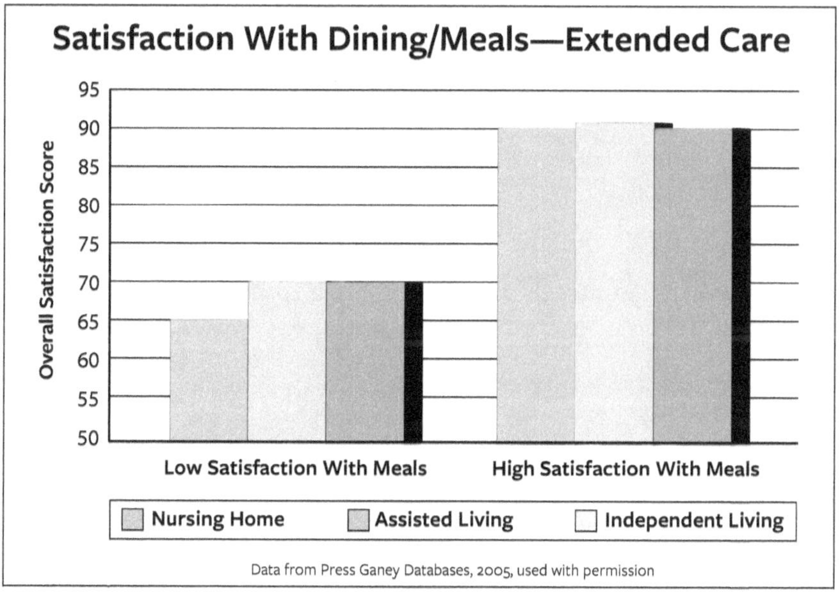

My master's research focused on this very aspect. There is an impact of hospitality and service on the dining experience for senior care community residents, and I saw that when I answered the call to become a dietary manager in 1987. I then decided it was worth studying when I embarked on this research in 2000.

When I began my master's studies, there was no research on customer service in long-term care facilities at that time. Hospitals had started to focus on customer service, and they introduced on-demand room service for the maternity ward, which was considered "groundbreaking."

Yet, even with working on the operations of this type of system, there was still a great lag in bringing meaningful service and relationships around dining into long-term care communities.

I thought to myself, *residents are not prisoners!* They should start having a choice of when to eat, where to eat, and what to eat. This was and is the beginning of person-centered hospitality.

And dining in senior living and post-acute care communities involves both the experience and the food. Food must be nutritious, culturally relevant, and served with kindness and skill. Taco night or a hot food buffet cannot overcome a staff member who is not attentive, respectful, or considerate. I've learned people are not born knowing how to build better relationships. They must have the opportunity to learn why and how when they step into this work. In doing so, they become critical community assets who support residents and the company that hired them.

This issue will be even more critical as we see an increase in residents[4] moving into communities specifically designed to meet and exceed the hospitality and service standards of older adults and their family members. My observations have shown that you can improve the quality of the food by as much as 80 percent by having staff that support a Kind Dining experience.

This important focus not only creates a hospitable environment for residents and staff but also improves health outcomes, job satisfaction, and resident and staff retention in the community. And that impacts the bottom line.

I am excited for you, the reader, to embark on this journey. As your guide, it is my hope that you will have moments of laughter, self-reflection, and transformation into how you personally show up when you are in the dining room. You may not believe it yet, but you are a vital component in that experience. Your presence matters to all.

Let's start by looking at why Kind Dining is critical.

PART I

Why Kind Dining Matters

The definition of well-being put forth by Merriam-Webster is a state of being happy, healthy, and prosperous.[5]

How will residents tell others about the quality of your community unless they enjoy their quality of life in that community?

How will they have a better quality of life if they do not enjoy their mealtimes in their new home?

How will they be treated kindly while dining if the server does not know how?

How are they to serve with kindness unless they have been taught?

And how will they be taught unless the provider's leadership makes the investment in hospitality training?

I was driving with my husband, and we had National Public Radio (NPR) tuned in. They started a story about sex in nursing homes. I immediately perked up because my business is in nursing homes and senior living/post-acute care communities.

The story went on to share that the communities had to set very specific standards and policies regarding romance, including training staff so they would know how to handle certain situations. So, I turned to my husband and said, "If I can make dining as tantalizing as sex, then I could be on NPR!"

Dining is an intimate experience and involves being open to connection, discovery, and unity around this common goal. It is personal and close—it evokes emotion. What emotion are you creating when you set the table, converse with a coworker, serve a plate of food, or assist a resident to eat ?

The manner in which staff show up in the dining room can affect the entire day's experience for the resident. And each meal provides a choice of whether to connect or to isolate. This is so much more than just providing a nutritious, hot meal. This is about showing dignity, respect, and compassion in a person's home because the dining room in that community is where people gather.

I would invite all readers to think about a similar experience they have encountered when consuming a meal, both at home and in a restaurant. What did you come away with in that experience, and what could have been done differently? This book will provide many aha moments for you. It can also help you to reflect on how you can develop curiosity about this approach.

And the approach is inherently different and will make you feel more in control of daily routines and ultimately, your destiny. Learning new skills will help you make more of the moments in your job, find more purpose, get along better with residents and colleagues, and discover more opportunities that you never knew existed.

My definition of hospitality is an attitude where we treat others with kindness, generosity, and love. Everyone knows what kindness and generosity feel like. But what do I mean by love in this particular context?

Love in this context is centered on civility. This does not mean the absence of rudeness. Not being rude is only being neutral, not civil. Civility is an intentional choice to help others from our hearts to theirs. And the dining experience, because it is a universal one that every person can relate to, is the best place to start to bring in civility and hospitality into our communities and our lives.

Let's start by reviewing six truths about how dining can impact a community and its reputation and, ultimately, the success of that organization.

1

Six Truths About Dining's Role In Community Marketplace Success Or Failure

The role of dining has become increasingly important in senior living and post-acute care communities. Residents consider their community their home, and they not only demand respect but have earned it.

These six truths about dining and the role they play in the community's success or failure are not new, yet they are worth repeating.[6]

Truth #1: Mealtimes Market Your Community

There are a few things that residents and their families can review and compare when choosing a senior living or post-acute care community. They expect the staff and quality of care to be excellent. They expect the housing to be comfortable and safe.

One aspect where a community can shine is with the experience of the meal. In fact, studies have shown that both the food service and their impression of the staff factor significantly into their decision to choose a senior living or post-acute care community.[7]

I'm not talking about the marketing department's showcase of lunches or dinners for potential clients. I'm talking about the marketing that happens every time one of your staff members interacts with a resident while serving a meal. In each venue, every meal, every day. There are a thousand touchpoints daily.

The question then becomes, are you investing in positive marketing or inadvertently investing in negative marketing?

A positive experience in this area goes far beyond better resident health outcomes. Families will show up more to dine with their family members. And they will share that dining experience with others, regardless of whether those individuals are actively searching for senior living and post-acute care options.

Many times, the marketing department will upsell the food quality and availability to the end user. A marketing department may say, "You can have filet mignon." They might inadvertently oversell the menu without checking with the food service department. These teams end up practicing self-sabotage instead of clearly communicating facts versus aspirations. The reality has to match the presentation and what's possible.

Every marketing team member and HR staff member should be trained on the menu and what is possible in the dining room. Unfortunately, this does not always happen. This is where well-trained food servers can step in and make the service and hospitality more in alignment with expectations. This helps bridge the possible expectation gap in the dining experience. However, having all staff understand the dining experience in your community is paramount, so the servers are not constantly put in that position.

As I shared earlier, research shows residents who are happy eating in your community also enjoy living there more.[8] While the marketing department needs to fully understand the menu and manage expectations, employees need to be on the same page on the value of a positive dining experience and the impact this experience has on marketing the overall community success.

How do you know this is not happening in your community?

One of the first things that can easily be taught and will improve the quality of the food and the experience is to train staff on how to support your current menu and food quality offered. Do you have a policy that states that your staff cannot talk badly about the food, especially in front of your residents?

At the very least, they can taste the food to see what items they enjoy. Sadly, they don't often get that option without management support. In the most successful communities, the food servers and ancillary staff are trained to sample the menu so they can talk about it accurately. In doing so, they can make small modifications or offer reasonable alternatives to ensure the resident enjoys every meal. This empowers the staff to be more hands-on and have both the ability and the opportunity to provide a stellar experience.

Communities fall short when they think that serving meals is equivalent to meal delivery and not a hospitality experience every single time. It is a hospitality experience in each venue and level of care, no matter which department oversees the dining service. Each organization has the opportunity to succeed and excel when it aligns its business strategy with an intentional focus on the one area its clients universally value: mealtimes.

Truth #2: Residents Can Spend 60 Percent Of Their Day Focused On Meals

Consequently, so do many of your staff. The dining room is more than where residents sit down to consume a meal. This is also where they have the opportunity to socialize and meet new people. For some, this is one of the few times during the day that they leave their apartment.

While I was doing my graduate research, residents shared with me that mealtime was when they found out who was now streaking their hair with the color pink, who went to the doctor's, anxious to tell us the result, and who was ready to entertain us with their fish stories. These are the moments when people bond. Family visits can be sparse in this busy world, so other residents fill the daily space that families once filled. Coming from different backgrounds, cultures, and places is now a point of interest, not a separating factor.

Interplay with the staff is vital. It is the staff members who take the place of family, in that they can draw out new residents who are too shy to be on their own by personally introducing them to others. The staff may think they are too busy to interact with residents because they have other duties throughout the day, but the mealtime block is an important nurturing role they should embrace.

A caregiver who happened to sit next to me during a flight shared a story with me.

> "My client moved into an assisted living facility," she said. "For the next twenty years, she ate alone in her room. This resulted from the first day she arrived in the dining room. She went to sit at one table and was told, 'You can't sit here, I am holding it for a friend.' She walked over to another table with empty chairs and was told the same thing. My client was so embarrassed,

> feeling rejected, that she went to her room and never set foot in the dining room again."

A well-trained staff member would have avoided this painful situation, would have known the key person to introduce her to, and would have saved time and money by not having to send staff to deliver meals to her room. Unfortunately, the unhappy resident could not leave this community, but I'll bet she didn't recommend it to anyone else either.

In truth #1, I mentioned that dining is very important when people decide whether to move into your community. I'll mention here that it is even more critical in determining whether or not to stay. Research shows that once residents move in and get settled, *dining becomes the second most important factor* in their overall satisfaction.

Vital Research polled assisted living communities.[9] In the residents' eyes, only administration is considered more important than dining—not competence, activities, or even the environment they live in.

I had a conversation with Vivian Tellis-Nayak, a respected expert in customer service research in LTC communities, who shared that "high satisfaction with the dining experience wins over residents and family members. They, in turn, are more likely to recommend a community."

Validating higher satisfaction with the dining experience leads to more referrals and move-in opportunities.

Have you ever had a resident or two leave because they were frustrated by poor service, whether in dining or housekeeping, or a new community opened down the street?

When a resident leaves, you're paying to refurbish their apartment, adding marketing costs, advertising, and administrative expenses. Current research[10] shows that the average monthly cost for rent in a senior care community is around $5,000. In some instances, it could take up to sixty days to redo the apartment and have a new resident come in. All in, the revenue loss could reach $15,000 per resident lost.

In today's competitive marketplace, losing a resident to another community is an expense you can't afford. Happy residents don't move out. Happy residents brag about their community and invite friends to come for lunch.

And let's face it: When residents move in, they are not grading your community on your kitchen or dining room makeover.

My question to you is: How many of your direct care servers or frontline foodservice staff, full- and part-time, understand that poor service affects so many aspects of a resident's quality of life?

Knowledge comes from combining formal education and hands-on experience, and from learning quickly that management is a significant factor in working with staff and residents. It is a team effort. Every thought, word, and deed is vital in creating a balance.

Traditionally, our concentration on meals and food service has been more about the quality of the food. In the future, it will be about the quality of hospitality and service.

Truth #3: There Is A Gap Between Expectations And Service Delivery

As customers, we make many assumptions about how we are being treated (it may not be the intention of the server or anyone delivering a service). However, our perceptions are our reality.

How about your resident expectations?

I have always believed the interactions between staff and residents in senior living and post-acute care communities are service encounters, whether it is in dining, housekeeping, or having a shower.

Throughout my career, I have often been critiqued for this very thinking. I have never understood the logic behind not treating residents as customers.

Part of my rationale could be that I never worked within the medical model mindset of service delivery, which is quite a different way of thinking.

Residents are having higher expectations for the service and hospitality they receive at mealtimes in post-acute and senior living communities across the board. Staff members can no longer be left untrained and ignorant. Service quality can make the difference between whether a resident moves in, stays, or leaves, and what they say about your community.

Staff often do not realize how important their service is to the future success of the company. Many staff serving meals told me during my research that they believe they don't have time to provide "service." They often say that when they feel under pressure, they will "sacrifice polite, courteous behavior." *Do you ever see that happen?*

When a new potential resident visits the community with their family, they will often linger in the dining room. They wish to see how the staff interacts with the residents, as well as see what types of food are being served. And believe me, those visitors can tell very quickly what kind of service is being provided.

The gap may not happen so obviously in the independent dining room, but it can and does happen in the assisted living and memory care environments. More staff are required when there is a greater need for eating assistance. And having a keen eye for individual residents plays a large role.

I remember one instance where a caregiver was cueing a resident to eat. The registered dietitian happened to be in the dining room and commented to the server, "This resident is left-handed, and you are asking her to eat with her right hand. That might be why she is struggling." Details matter.

Also, with everything being digital at this point, a visitor could capture a less-than-stellar moment, and that bad press could spread like wildfire. Unwilling or uneducated staff is no longer an excuse for not meeting higher expectations.

It's time to dissolve the gap between the residents expecting to receive high-quality service and the staff unwilling or untrained to provide it.

Truth #4: There Is A Continued Focus On Higher Quality Of Service And Care

How are you delivering? With the Centers for Medicare & Medicaid Services federal guidelines stressing a person-centered approach to senior care,[11] those aging into a senior-living community also want a much higher standard of service.

You can have fewer staff if they are adequately trained. They instinctively know what needs to be done and work together as a cohesive unit to accomplish those tasks. And they understand the uniqueness of each resident.

This is a room full of individuals with experiences and stories that make each of them unique and an important part of the community. Residents want much more say in their dining experience. They want to select the food that reminds them of past experiences, including travel and visits to a variety of restaurants. They also want to continue to celebrate events around the table. Even though they are now living in a senior community, they still want that personalization and freedom of choice.

Truth #5: You're Dependent On Your Lowest-Paid, Least-Trained Staff To Manage Your Most Important Experience

Let that sink in for a second. You are handing off one of the most significant opportunities for experience and word-of-mouth marketing to some of your least trained staff. These employees are being held responsible for creating relationships that are so critical to resident and family satisfaction. They, in essence, are the conduit between management, the kitchen, and the customer (i.e., the resident and families).

Just because they are lower-paid does not mean they are not vital to the community's success. As we've mentioned, they are central figures to dining quality. Investment in their education on social skills and how to build lasting interpersonal relationships is rarely provided in senior care communities. When it is, and coupled with the creation of clear and concise service standards, it instructs staff members how best to interact with residents and one another. Their success becomes vital to the success of your community and can provide substantial return on investment and a competitive edge.

Some communities focus on investing instead on remaking the dining room, adding a happy hour, or another quick fix. Those gimmicks cannot replace a strong dining experience. Someone once told me in reference to poorly trained servers, "It's like building a Formula 1 race car and putting the Little Old Lady from Pasadena behind the wheel."

You may think I am referring to the kitchen staff. What I am really talking about is any person in any department who serves a meal and is part of this equation. Generally, the caregiving staff do not receive customer service/hospitality training. And these are the staff members who benefit the most from this type of training.

Some may say, "I was not hired to be a waitress." I am not asking them to become a waitress. What I am asking, and what you should also be asking, is for them to take the dining experience and make it a powerful tool for connection, community, and caring.

Caregivers are often not told they will spend half their day serving food. But this is part of providing care and service to the residents. They, and their direct supervisors, need to truly understand how important the dining environment is, and how they play a critical role as well.

Truth #6: This Last Truth Is The Culmination Of The Other Truths—You Must Invest In Your People

What are you missing out on if you choose not to? Professional training and development create camaraderie between employees. It aligns the different departments together and helps them work toward a collective goal.

It also fosters trust and consistency, where employees believe in their worth and feel they can positively impact the community and its residents. *They stay.* And we learn from *The Calling: Why Healthcare Is So Special*[12] by author Quint Studer that people are drawn to post-acute care and senior living because they have a heart for helping and being useful.

According to a study published in *Harvard Business Review*,[13] a thriving workforce is one where employees are not just satisfied and productive but also engaged in creating both their future and the future of the company. And thriving employees have a bit of an edge. They actually care.

A well-known adage is that good service can save a bad meal, but a good meal cannot save bad service. When you go out to eat and you spend money, you also expect great service to be part of that equation. You want high value for your dollar. Your residents are going "out" to eat, sometimes every single day. Do you think they are any different?

A well-known adage is that good service can save a bad meal, but a good meal cannot save bad service.

How Training Impacts The Value Chain

The value chain is the revenue of the community, where you have a customer (the resident) who pays money. They continue to pay money and even invite other people to become customers because they're satisfied with the service.

Some people may think that residents are real estate customers, but they are not. The vast majority are investing in a life experience, which includes the staff, the other residents, and an important conduit: food. It is a universal language of love, satisfaction, and belonging.

What makes residents satisfied with the service is when the staff who serve them are also happy and satisfied. And what makes them happy and satisfied? They are most happy with their job when they have a good relationship with their immediate supervisor and with the people they work with daily. Finally, if they feel that the work they do is important, they think that they matter.

Investment in consistent professional training helps to make the six truths work for the community and elevate the dining experience. It provides the foundation for more pride in the work we do serving older adults, for better relationships with our colleagues and our customers (again, the residents), and for making what we do, even something as small as making sure ketchup comes with the hot fries, impactful.

Training matters if you are serious about positively impacting your residents' nutritional health and well-being and your business's bottom line.[14] What does that missed opportunity between connection and community look like?

2

The Missed Civility Opportunity Of Connection And Community

It's not just about the food.

Let me say that again, because you may have missed it. It's not *just* about the food.

There is typically enough time, appreciation, money, and talent to make a great meal. But what can impact any meal is how it is served. Is it served with the idea of connection and community in mind? Or is it just a task that a server wants to get through quickly to get onto other "important" items in their day? This is where civility, when added appropriately, elevates the entire community and creates amazing environments.

Asking someone to hand someone a plate of food, even if it is hot, well prepared, and exactly what was ordered, is a missed opportunity if we don't include the choice of civility. This is where we can focus on the whole community, not just one single plate of food.

When you hand someone an aspirin, it is a different relationship than when you are serving them a piece of their favorite apple pie. There is a universal connection that can happen in that moment, but only if it is chosen. Otherwise, it is merely a job to be completed.

Time To Meet Your Tour Guide

Before you take a guided tour of Kind Dining, you should meet your tour guide. This is how my quest to improve the quality of life for older adults living in residential communities began.

After owning restaurants in Alaska, working as a dietary manager in a large nursing home, and serving as a food service director in assisted living/retirement communities in Portland, Oregon, I was hired by Sysco, the giant foodservice distributor, as a health care specialist in 1989.

I went into this work with ideas to *improve the dining experience*, having fully understood the daily grind, rewards, and balance of foodservice and nursing teams serving hundreds of meals to a vulnerable population, with whom I fell in love. It was a job and a career that spanned seventeen years. As part of my responsibilities, I worked directly with corporate healthcare providers, executive directors, department managers, chefs, nutrition professionals, and frontline teams to oversee food quality and create menu programs that satisfied all stakeholders.

But something was wrong. Change would not come easily. The older adults that I loved were the victims of undeserved misfortune. No one had taught the industry how important food is to people living in an isolated setting. And it is not just about the food, but the relationships around it. Mealtime (it was not even called dining yet) was handled in a haphazard, sometimes downright rude way at residential care communities.

Attention was not being paid to how residents want pleasant interaction at mealtimes. This was becoming a quality-of-life issue, with food merely being dispensed and not served. To really create change, I would need to teach community-serving staff how they could make a difference, and people at the top, why it mattered, so I went back to school for a master's degree.

In 2000, I met Professor Ann Messersmith, PhD, RD, LD. She was the head of the Department of Nutrition and Food Management at Oregon State University (OSU). She was starting one of the first distance-delivered dietetic management master's programs in the country. I told her about my *big* dream and mission to enhance the nutritional health and well-being of older adults living in communities by improving the dining experience worldwide.

Through my observations working in communities, I could see how residents' cognition improved, as well as their disposition, when I supplied them with what they wanted to eat more often. It was worth heated conversations with nurses and executives over the size of a piece of chocolate cake for a resident with diabetes and the food budget, respectively. I was knowledgeable in diet and disease interactions and talented enough to teach my kitchen staff to make items from scratch to stretch the budget.

We both understood that it was not going to be easy, but she believed in my purpose to change the dining culture in senior living and post-acute care. And she said something that put me on the path to Kind Dining: "To have the most impact, you need to learn instructional design, build a training that changes behavior, and start a movement in retraining healthcare leadership and frontline teams."

In 2005, I received a master's degree in nutrition and food management from OSU with this premise: *Best Practices In Customer Service–Oriented Meal Service In Long-Term Care*. About the same time, Sysco decided to reduce the number of product specialists, so I decided to depart the corporate world.

In 2006, I formed Higher Standards, LLC, a consulting and training company focused on making my research discoveries a reality in training. I hired a top-notch instructional designer, built and piloted Kind Dining training with three local, yet nationally known, lifecare communities, and set out to teach, train, and speak around the country. My big ambition was to one day train one thousand senior living and post-acute care communities on how they can use the dining experience as the most cost-effective method to also deliver dignity, community, and kindness to both residents and staff caring for them.

I wish I could simply say that the next year, I reached my goal. It took persistence, and I had to endure several obstacles along the way to making Kind Dining a movement.

First, my company survived the recession of 2008 to 2010 and the pandemic of 2020 to 2023. Eighteen years later, after training dozens and dozens of communities, I got an email that forever changed my trajectory.

It turns out that several key staff at DiningRD had been following my journey. DiningRD was looking for a training series specifically designed to serve older adults in post-acute care and senior living communities to help their clients train staff and elevate their dining standards. DiningRD has an amazing community, including one thousand dietitians and nutrition professionals who represent eight thousand communities in the United States and now Canada.

The deal was struck in the spring of 2024, and DiningRD acquired Higher Standards, LLC and Kind Dining training. My original goal of this training, which was to reach one thousand communities, was achieved and then some.

So much has been improved in the dining experience with the culture change phenomenon and person-centered/directed care focus over the last twenty-five years, but there are still three gaps in dining service for older adults that need to be closed, which I recognized while conducting my graduate research in 2004:

1. Serving staff, from all departments, are untrained in creating a personal, holistic experience from the residents' perspective.
2. Both staff and residents are experiencing incivility daily.
3. There is limited understanding and appreciation from staff serving meals for what the dining experience offers for overall community success.

This was in 2004, and these gaps persist. In fact, after all we have gone through these last few years with the pandemic, these gaps have not just widened but have contributed to the worldwide loneliness epidemic we are experiencing.

Currently, I am an unofficial Kind Dining ambassador and evangelist working with DiningRD. These are the service gaps that are near and dear to my heart and ones I want to see overcome. Today, there is an opportunity to reduce, and even eliminate, these gaps. And the frontline staff have the ball to take it over the finish line.

PART II

Nine Ways Frontline Staff Can Make A Difference For Resident Experiences

Terese Scollard gets pissed off when things fail. She is a retired registered dietitian and clinical nutrition manager, and I have known her for years. In the flow of patients that ended up under her care in the hospital, she could see the failures that cause older adults to be malnourished, even in a controlled setting like a hospital or rehab facility. Her whole career was focused on preventing those failures.

There are gaps that are systematic, such as not meeting or monitoring food intake and weight changes, muscle mass changes, declines in strength and physical function and other standards of care, as well as knowledge gaps with staff, such as not recognizing signs of weight loss, even in overweight people, and eating problems. The thing that stands out the most to Terese is the "massive weight loss" incidents that caused elderly patients to experience malnutrition and unintentional weight loss under medical "supervision." Someone didn't take or pass the wheel to another professional.

Ted was one of those patients living in a long-term care community, and Terese shared his story. He was 5'9" and weighed 213 pounds at the start of this story. He was an older man, overweight, and receiving treatment for cancer. He was relying on oral food intake to meet his nutritional needs and was losing weight, but was still considered overweight by BMI and his weight for height. His team of healthcare professionals did not react promptly to his symptoms, rate, and amount of weight loss, and the alert from a nutrition professional was missed.

He continued to lose weight on his oral diet for three months before someone figured out there was a nutrition problem, and the weight loss was abnormal and too rapid to be solely attributed to the chemotherapy.

When he was referred to a registered dietitian, she performed a nutritional assessment and said that he needed a tube feeding immediately. This means that he was so malnourished that he needed immediate intervention to prevent more serious health complications.

Ted was then admitted to the hospital and started on the tube feeding for only four days, which was inadequate because four days would not put a dent in replenishing a patient who had been steadily, in essence, in semi-starvation for three months. This was a very poor stopgap measure, and he ended up being readmitted.

So, what was the miss here? What should the care team have been looking for? Was he leaving food on his plate consistently? Should someone have noticed that, as he was coming off treatments, having symptoms that contributed to a poor food intake, he was not showing up at the dining room? When should the alarm bells have gone off? What should they have looked for with unintentional weight loss, especially with someone who is overweight yet severely malnourished?

Perhaps a frontline staff worker would have noticed that he didn't come down for meals or was quick to leave once he arrived. That person could have noticed that food was pushed around the plate to look like it was eaten or hidden in a napkin. Someone who was more attuned to Ted and his eating habits might have picked up on something sooner.

Not every resident encounter will end up being this extreme. But it also shows the dangers of being on autopilot when staff interact with residents at mealtimes. The key to preventing unintentional weight loss is good communication. Professionally trained serving staff are poised to be another set of eyes and ears for the nurses and doctors. After all, they may interact with the residents more in one day than the nurses do for the week.

And suppose we do not understand as employees two critical functions of our daily work. In that case, the first is our role in protecting the residents we serve (optimizing their quality of life), and the second is respecting the company that hired us. How do we commit to doing these two things if we are not taught?

During my graduate research, I conducted focus group meetings with residents and staff, looking at service priorities. There are three service gaps in creating communities of belonging that I believe any training will help close: staff are untrained in creating a personal and holistic experience; both staff and residents have experienced incivility; and there is little appreciation for the dining experience overall.

Each of these gaps focuses on the experience, real or imagined. Each of these gaps is also well within the scope of what a community can fix. However, staff have shared that fixing these gaps seems to be very difficult. What if there were ways that, with awareness, alignment, and actions, these gaps could close?

There are nine areas where all staff can develop skills to improve the quality of residents' health and well-being. Each of these provides a solid foundation in creating a civil community and eliminating these service gaps. And each is worthy of that noble pursuit.

3

Meals Provide Moments Of Connection

Nancy worked her way through nursing school by being a waitress at an upscale diner. One of the requirements of that job was to attend several sessions of customer service training, designed to make her more successful in her position. Classes were geared toward company culture and service standards.

She was proud of her exceptional ability to make her diners feel good, valued, and appreciated. And this paid off in her enjoyment of her work. When she graduated from nursing school, she went to work at a continuing care retirement community. She knew that her job was to improve the health and care of the residents from a medical vantage point. She also supervised care staff and certified nurse aides (CNAs) who served meals in the assisted living dining room. Unbeknownst to her, she had a blind spot.

I had an expectation of her that she had missed. In her mind, and in this context, it was not her job to worry about the meal service in the assisted living dining room, even though, when it was pointed out, she could clearly see that the staff was treating it as a hurried task. She knew that the staff were stuck, feeling under pressure, and didn't have the skills to make it easier. Plus, it never really mattered before.

Nancy had knowledge about how to serve better, to make people feel special while dining, but didn't realize that she could or should change that dining experience in her community.

We all have blind spots. By participating in a training workshop designed exclusively to meet the service expectations of older adults, Nancy had an epiphany and was reminded of the social relationship she has with residents. She never realized that her residents have dining service expectations and deserve to be treated with the same dignity, courtesy, and respect as any other diner in any other dining venue. She finally saw through applying new skills and a change of mindset that she was helping herself and her team make gathering around the table more comfortable for all.

Staff serving meals is the bridge between the residents and the company caring for them. Their attitude and approach toward mealtimes are powerful moments of opportunity for residents to feel special in their own right and cherished as members of an extended family living in a community. Staff can connect with why they personally chose to work in a particular community. And the community can demonstrate the value placed on them through proper training.

Not An Office But A Home

We have all had jobs where we go to an office, retail store, or other location. What makes senior living and post-acute care communities unique is that staff work in someone's home, not in a corporate building.

When we learn to *utilize the time spent interacting* around the table, with intentional focus, we actually help solidify our connections and show honor and respect while working in this environment. That focus results in feelings of belonging in the dining room and beyond, throughout the day.

When we understand the certain likes and dislikes that the residents have around the meal, we can introduce the meal and have a conversation. We can introduce residents to each other, with the main goal to help staff understand that, since we are working in someone's home, we have a responsibility to help them feel at home in that relationship.

Staff can oftentimes overlook just how valuable they are in that moment and in that relationship. Often, the staff serving meals may never have served before. This could be their first time actually presenting someone a meal.

The service aspect is becoming more and more important in the dining room. I've learned we are neither born nor often trained in the knowledge, skills, and attitudes necessary for us to be successful in this work. However, we all can learn a skill set in building better relationships, not just serving a meal.

This includes getting to know the residents more in that context so that they can build stronger relationships.

And what makes relationships work better? I believe having the attitude of hospitality in its purest form makes relationships work. Not only does it highlight relationships around the meal and identify the server's role as "the" responsible person in creating the best experience for the resident at each meal, but it is also an important virtue that can be applied to improve all our relationships.

By embracing new skills and a new mindset, staff can start to see the impact and the importance of the dining experience in a larger context.

We need to optimize the residents' quality of life and value our fellow employees to uphold the community and the company that hired us.

French Fries And No Ketchup

I was conducting focus group meetings with caregivers who served meals to understand more about their comprehension of residents' service expectations. One of the conversations focused on the choice the staff made when they were serving hamburgers and french fries.

If ketchup didn't come up with the cart delivering the hamburgers, they would tell the residents that they didn't serve ketchup today because it wasn't available. And the residents knew that wasn't the case.

The staff saw their job as serving as efficiently and as fast as possible. So that meant to make up an excuse why there was no ketchup served with french fries. There was a gap between what the staff was doing and what the residents expected. And residents expected ketchup to come with their fries.

Part of the issue was personalizing the experience. If they were eating out, would they expect ketchup to come with their fries? And if so, would they then also expect someone to get the missing ketchup?

This was my first realization that we might have a bigger issue than just ketchup—bad service happens on its own.

The staff here didn't take ownership of the missing ketchup because the kitchen didn't send it up. They didn't see themselves as being in the same context as a "server/waitperson" that the resident viewed them. They did not see themselves as an extension of the company they work for at that moment.

You represent many things, including the company and the residents' experience.

In addition to this overall problem, we also had to strategize on how to solve the issue of missing items. Could they keep condiments, including ketchup, close enough so that if a condiment was missing from a plate, they would have extra at hand? They didn't have to check each plate beforehand, but as they were serving, they could quickly glance at the plate and see whether there was ketchup included or not. And they had extra ready on the dolly to grab more if needed.

This strategy took an extra three to five minutes to ensure additional condiments were on hand and to quickly glance at a plate and remedy a missing item.

This also meant that staff could slow down when serving to make sure the resident had everything they needed without adding too much time.

The residents noticed the difference immediately. They didn't feel as if the staff was just throwing down food and rushing off. They took an extra few seconds to check in with the resident. Those few seconds allowed for a quick connection. And this opened up additional moments to make sure they were enjoying their meal.

Connection can happen in moments of caring and serving, and meals provide plenty for both staff and residents, if they know how to take the time to find and use those moments—knowing how makes the difference between training and trying.

Creating Moments For Sharing And Making Lifelong Relationships

I was making coffee in one of the nursing homes, staring at the machine and lost in thought. I had a flashback to False Island and the need for patience, curiosity, flexibility, and kindness as the young adults who were working there were adjusting to being away from home. I was able to connect with how the residents could be feeling homesick for their former homes, freedom, and lives.

False Island in Alaska is in a very remote wilderness location. In 1980, it was a primitive (no phones, no electricity, no stores nearby) logging camp converted into a Young Adult Conservation Corps (YACC) residential camp, run by the U.S. Forest Service. I was hired to run the food service operation, feeding fifty to one hundred people daily, who were recruited from all over the country. They didn't know each other when they arrived. Many were away from home for the first time. Many were experiencing loneliness and isolation, even in a camp full of people.

I didn't understand this at first, as I was so focused on my own responsibilities. In fact, I often saw their complaints as a distraction. Of course, they felt homesick and missed their regional and home-cooked comfort foods. I didn't know what I could do about it until the idea hit me.

To try to combat this and learn more about them, I brought two corps members a day into the kitchen on rotation. I had to focus on what they were experiencing at that moment. They were hungry for food, family, friends, and the homes they left.

By inviting them into the kitchen, we got to know one another. They began to learn some culinary skills—e.g., baking bread (sourdough, of course), cookies, pies, specialty granola—and preparing meals from scratch, as well as growing a garden. They became comfortable enough to share incredible stories and family recipes. We created a tight-knit community and family of forever False Islanders. I still am in contact with many of those members and staffers nearly five decades later, and the stories they now share from their vast experience are nothing short of inspirational.

I learned how important comfort food becomes to people living in an isolated setting, whether it's serving young adults in the wilderness or older adults in post-acute care and senior living.

My survival motto became, "Feed them what they want." Now that may sound very basic and simplistic, but sometimes the fundamentals of getting along are the most important thing and need to be revisited often. It's not just about the food—it's about the relationship around it. To the Wisconsinites, butter was their farm back home. For those from Southern California, granola represented love. The food brought them back to the relationships they were missing.

What I hope for with this training is for you to find connection in conversation around the table and beyond, and to help spark a fire in you to do more. This requires a change in mindset along with a sense of unity as we build something better together.

False Island taught me that hospitality doesn't apply just to lodging or restaurants, but also to how we greet others. We can create safe places of acceptance and love in all of our interactions, from parents and children, wives and husbands, teachers and students, healers and patients.

The attitude of hospitality is as ancient as the Golden Rule. There is inherent value in teaching lifelong skills. One does not need to be famous or wealthy to share the gift of hospitality.

Integrating Head, Hands, And Heart

It is critical in this journey to understand the value of dining together. When people gather, they want to feel connected. Sitting together doesn't mean that they know each other. What are you observing, and what are you assuming? And how can you help? Remember, if residents are happy eating in your community, they like living there more. How can you make this the best experience for the residents?

We can start with something simple. Have you ever thought about how you come across while serving meals? Are you rushed or relaxed? Happy or annoyed? You can start by observing your actions in your community and how that impacts what is happening in your dining room. This is an invitation to move away from looking at what you do as a task and instead look at how you are impacting the lives of the residents.

If you see something that needs improvement, you can talk to your manager, a coworker, or even a Kind Dining trainer, if you have one. The goal is to identify what you can change (in the community and in yourself).

You are working in their home where they should feel safe, secure, and loved. You set the ambiance, making the space inviting and welcoming to all. And it is up to you to respect the residents, the company you work for, and the product you are serving.

As you serve the meal, are you embodying the company's mission with every plate? Do you know what your organization's values are? How can you impact their delivery every day? You also have a personal mission statement—define that narrative and understand your actions show that mission every time you show up for work. You are the face of the organization. Residents view the organization through how you act and how you treat others.

4

Aging Wisdom Transforms Perspectives

I got a huge surprise in one of my training classes, where I was teaching younger adults.

Many of them are in their first job serving meals to residents. And one of the teenagers, Marina, said to me, “Old people scare me.”

Wow. Here she is in her first job in assisted living. So, I asked her, “What do you do when an older person approaches you?”

And she says, “I just turn around and walk away.”

She was afraid and didn’t know how to connect with residents because she didn’t know what to say. So, instead of focusing on what she should say, we practiced her asking questions to the residents.

What Marina discovered is that there were amazing stories to be uncovered in each conversation. Instead of focusing on being uncomfortable, she sought something interesting about each person. One resident had written a novel. One had been a professional singer. One had traveled the world and had amazing stories to share. Another had ten children and twenty-eight grandchildren. She would not have found out these facts if she had not made the effort to connect.

Getting to grow older is a gift we take for granted as young people. The words of wisdom we hear from elders often evade us until we least expect them. We suddenly grow to the age where it makes sense.

Look at your own perspective of being alive and envision how you want to be treated as you age. Latch on to the opportunity to change the shape of aging for the future.

The Gift Of Age

Who are you serving? You are serving individuals with a history and stories to tell. It is an amazing process to grow older. Often, we don't appreciate the phases of aging residents are going through because we haven't thought about them.

If you haven't had a relationship with a grandparent, you may assume that we're meeting these people at a different stage of life. You may not realize that they were young once themselves and have lived amazing lives.

As part of your job, you have the honor of knowing the people that you're serving. If this were a relative of yours, like a grandparent, great-aunt, or great-uncle, how would you treat them in this situation? And are you treating someone that you don't yet know differently? This is more than knowing their medical histories. You have the opportunity to learn about their past and their experiences that make them who they are today.

Think of it this way: Fifty years ago, some of these people were teenagers. They could have gone to Elton John concerts or worked at a camp in Alaska where they helped bake bread and make granola (my story from my youth), or raced cars like my mom.

In remembrance of Bill and Evelyn Sullivan, Cindy's parents in 1951

As I age, one of my missions is to help people understand that they can learn a lot by engaging with older adults. And in any job that you will go into, you will more than likely have to work with older people. You have this opportunity to learn how to communicate and be empathetic with people as they age. Because no matter what job you go into, an older generation will be there. Learning these skills will, by far, increase your knowledge, professionalism, and life skills.

There are introverted residents as well as extroverted residents. Some of the extroverts would love to tell you their story and would like a listening ear. By the same token, some introverts would like to hear about your life.

Growing older is not a gift that every person gets. Keep that in mind as you work with older adults. They have witnessed incredible advancements, been eyewitnesses to history, and accomplished great things in their lifetimes.

Living Through World War I

Susan can remember the stories her grandmother would share about living through WWI when she was a young girl in Poland. She can recount the story her grandmother told her when she and her two younger brothers were taken from their home to work in the field picking crops.

"My grandmother would hide some of the food they were harvesting in her stockings so she could feed herself and her siblings," Susan shared. "She would talk to me about the hardship and also when they found joy in small things, like feeding a small squirrel."

Her grandmother taught Susan about perseverance and never giving up hope with these stories. "She was so resilient. It was because of what she endured during WWI that she decided to come to the US at only seventeen, alone, to start a new life. She worked three jobs when she was a young wife and mother. She taught me that hard work can pay off, and I bring that mentality into my career every day."

Susan was a role model in how not only to survive, but to thrive: "She worked at the Sunkist Pie Company in Chicago and taught me how to make pies from scratch. And it was in her small kitchen that she shared these stories—peeling apples and making the pie crust from scratch. Even now, the smell of apple pie brings me right back to that kitchen and those amazing conversations."

Many of our aging adults have a fear of being overlooked, dismissed, and not seen. If we take the story of Marina and review it from the viewpoint of that elderly resident, those fears could easily come up. No matter what, we should always treat our residents with dignity, respect, and love. When you become "old," how will you want others to treat you? What fears may come up for you at that age? It can be difficult, as there are fewer opportunities for interacting with the elderly population, even though we are becoming a society of older adults.

Those over sixty used to reluctantly face retirement. Today, they are looking forward to an age when they can set new goals and achieve new things. Diana Nyad, at sixty-nine years old, is the only person to swim from Florida to Cuba without a shark cage. Frank McCourt wrote his first book, a bestseller, after he retired from thirty years of teaching. Well-known actor Estelle Getty was in her sixties when she won her first Emmy.

Older adults now have the time to do what *they* want without the usual duties and obligations to derail those desires. What's more, they have accumulated wisdom, confidence, and social skills. Many have chosen to live in post-acute and senior living communities for that lifestyle change. Their challenge, and yours, is to help them connect with the community and continue to share their adventures.

Integrating Head, Hands, And Heart

Your work is important to every resident in your community every single day. You have an opportunity to impact the well-being of others in what you choose to focus on when you are doing that important work.

This isn't just about making sure residents are fed and have a place to eat. This is about the quality of life each person experiences. What you choose to do every day can either build the community up or tear it down. And that choice is yours to make every time you step into the building. This includes the respect you give to older adults and their life experiences.

Are you greeting residents using their names as they approach you and including a smile and direct eye contact? Are you taking the time to learn something about each person in your care? If you have an events calendar, can you talk about the upcoming events with the residents? Are you appreciative of what the residents have gone through to get to this stage in their lives? And as an older adult, how would you like to be treated?

Becoming more comfortable with personal interactions is helpful in your work here. You have a front-row seat to amazing life stories and lessons from the people you meet every day. These experiences cannot be duplicated or replaced. When you can look at interactions with the aging population in your community positively, it is a gift.

5

Work Shapes Personal Growth

Dan's story is a tale of the underdog that made it. He started as a dishwasher in a long-term care center. He approached the job initially as nothing special. For him, it was just a job, and he was washing dishes. Then he started going out and bussing tables in the dining room. Because of that addition he made to the job, he started interacting with residents and getting to know them a little bit.

As time went by, he realized that he enjoyed bussing tables and those conversations with residents. He felt he wanted to put in a genuine effort into this work and maybe advance his career in this community. And so, he went from being a busboy to looking at becoming a caregiver. Because of that focus, he decided to return to school and pursue some training.

Community colleges offer programs to become a nurse aide. That was his next stepping stone. From there, he decided to go into administration and become an administrator for this community.

For Dan, there was a nobility in working with the residents. Dan started as a high school graduate who just wanted a job. He went from just making a paycheck to making a difference. He saw that he could improve the lives of the seniors living there. And that was his career quest.

So, how did his story end? He became an administrator of the assisted living community where he started as a dishwasher.

Every Position Counts As An Opportunity

Every job we have in our career shapes who we are and who we will become. Being open to seeing this work as a stepping stone or as an opportunity to grow personally and professionally will pay off. Improving our skills in connecting with our residents, co-workers, and management will help us feel better about ourselves and what we bring to the workplace each day. Good communication and teamwork skills serve us well in all aspects of our lives. We are not born knowing the finer points of getting along.

What skills do you bring to the table, and how can you learn and grow? There are characteristics that the company is looking for and residents are looking for in terms of people caring for them. It is important to know what your strengths are and what your weaknesses are. It is a powerful tool in understanding how you can contribute to the success of the residents and the organization.

If you have an opportunity to complete any self-assessment, you will learn what your strengths and weaknesses are. You can focus on your strengths to improve at what you do best. And we can't all be good at the same thing, otherwise nothing would get done. By playing to your strengths and recognizing others' strengths, you can work together to build a team. Yes, you can focus on improving your weaknesses, and building up your strengths is also vital.

And whether you take the Kind Dining training with the available self-assessments or you find self-assessments online, there is still a great deal of value in understanding your core strengths that accelerate your personal development and learning what weaknesses are holding you back.

Leading By Example

I knew a kitchen aide, Maggie, who had worked in the kitchen for some time. She decided that she wanted to become a caregiver. There was a bit of animosity between the kitchen and the nursing staff. In this hierarchy, for the most part, the kitchen people are at the lower end of the totem pole.

Often, caregivers don't respect that meals start at a specific time. What Maggie decided to do was show that she can motivate and care for her residents in such a way that they would want to be in the dining room on time. She understood what the kitchen was going through when that didn't happen. Not only did she help the residents be on time, but she also helped them look their best.

She would make an extra effort to do someone's hair, dress them nicely, and make sure they're happy to go into the dining room. This had such an amazing impact on the other CNAs because they weren't taking the time to do that. Her actions inspired them to make more of an effort to get their residents ready for mealtime. And that led to a notable change in getting people to the dining room on time, and everybody looked their best.

Maggie learned something else in this process. There is a lot of teamwork in the kitchen to get the meal out on time. She noticed that the CNAs didn't operate that way. When they finished their work, they did not offer to help one another. She inspired a breakthrough there as well.

Being Recognized As A Whole

The OPTIMA Award is one of the highest recognitions a senior care community can get. The national award honors the most prestigious communities that focus on the experience of all to ensure a very high standard of hospitality and care.

Applying for the award takes a lot of work, not to mention the dedication of the community to improve group performance. The creation of a common purpose, an inclusion-based atmosphere, and the showcasing of this environment for the award impact the entire community. Each staff member must be dedicated to achieving the goal and showing up every day in pursuit of this noble goal.

Part of the journey for achieving the OPTIMA recognition is to have the opportunity to train and learn. By learning together, senior living and post-acute care communities are able to grow and thrive together. This helps shift the mindset of the entire group, which leads to sustainable change. Each staff member has a role to play in this movement.

Not only does working lead to personal growth, but so does working together toward an organizational goal, a standard of excellence, and an individual career milestone. There is often a bonus of increased family and guest meal revenue.

And the work we do together benefits the community in numerous ways. Several of the senior living and post-acute care communities that have taken the Kind Dining training have reported less employee turnover and an increase in their outside visitor dining revenue. In fact, one community saw its outside visitor dining revenue nearly double in the first year alone.

Many workers who went on to other opportunities or training would return to the community to continue to provide exceptional service.

When approached in a thoughtful manner and including training for all support staff, the hospitality aspect of the dining room became a beacon, attracting the right talent and best behaviors.

Integrating Head, Hands, And Heart

Do you have an opportunity where you work to gain new knowledge, skills, and attitudes? If you are not sure, this is a great time to ask so that you can learn and have moments to be taught.

There cannot be an "us versus them" mentality in any post-acute care and senior living community. We are part of an entire team, where each individual has career experiences that can make the group perform better. This includes leading by example and continually working to improve how you perform for your team, your community, and yourself.

By showing up to work each day with a "learner" mentality, you will embrace new challenges, learn new skills, and encourage team members to do the same. If we are able to conduct a self-assessment, we will discover what our strengths are and be sure to lean into those strengths for the good of the community.

There is a focus on the LEARN model[15] (Listen, Empathize, Ask Questions, Restate, New Behavior). While the first four steps of this model are all important, if we do not accompany them with new behaviors, we are bound to repeat the same process and get the same results.

No matter where we are in the organization or on our career path, there is always an opportunity to grow and develop. And when we support each other and the organization in that work, we can find additional tools to improve our service and make the residents happy that they have chosen our community. And it is a choice every single day.

There will be days when we are not at our best. This can be particularly true when there is a shortage of staff or resources. That doesn't mean that you should not do your best work and encourage those around you to do the same. By staying positive, we can set an example for others and minimize complaining or gossiping.

6

Preparation Speaks Volumes On Service Commitment

Helen was in a wheelchair and considered legally blind. She was comfortably wheeled up to the table, looking forward to lunch. The first thing she does when she arrives is to feel for her utensils. Her place setting was not complete—the fork was missing.

She felt frustrated and disappointed. Now she's going to have to flag someone down to bring a fork, which will call more attention to herself.

When she was telling me the story, the first thing that she said was, "I wish I weren't blind."

I use this as a teachable moment. If the fork had been there, she would have been confident and ready to go. That lack of preparation made a difference in her whole approach to the meal.

When I shared with staff why it matters to know how to set the table correctly every time and anticipate individual residents' needs, they responded with, "Cindy, it's just a fork."

But it's not about the fork. It's about the entire emotional aspect and the frustration that she felt. In her way of thinking, somebody was too busy or didn't care enough to make sure the setting was ready for her.

If no one explains the importance of residents' underlying emotions to staff, they do not know their behaviors could be creating a problem at all. This is an example of a hidden issue that brings negativity into the environment but one that can easily be fixed with training and communication.

First Impressions Are Powerful

Here is a secret: Getting ready to provide great service is nine-tenths of the event itself. And as we discussed earlier, residents look at mealtime as the highlight of the day. The joy that a happy dining room atmosphere brings, as good serving skills are executed, is priceless. The flow of the meal falters without good preparation. Residents often perceive that the lack of preparation and execution means we don't care enough about them to get it right. It is not our intention to convey this message, but it is the message we send.

When residents and family members come into the dining room, they have an immediate first impression of how the ambiance feels, how the tables look, how the room smells, and how it's lit up. The defining key in this healthcare setting is making sure that the table is set to the company standards and double-checked for the resident's expectations, focusing on their unique needs.

When we don't put their needs first, some residents react and let their frustration be known, sometimes taking it out on staff. Or they may say nothing, feel more alone, and think that it's not worth the effort to complain or burden the staff. In the story above, Helen was mad. Once they brought her the fork, she still didn't like the meal because she was hurt. And it took extra time and patience for her to feel comfortable and loved.

If someone (perhaps the staffer who set her wheelchair in place) was knowledgeable and accountable to help double-check the surrounding environment—if they had taken a few extra seconds to check and correct the place setting—Helen would have had a very different experience, and the staff would have as well.

Missing Out On Connection

I was flying to a conference, and I was sitting next to a gal who was a caregiver for an elderly woman. She worked privately for her, and she was her caregiver for twenty-five years. She shared this story, "The woman that I care for moved into an assisted living community. She went into the dining room for the very first time, and she went to sit at a table and was told she couldn't sit in that seat. And so, she thought, 'Oh, okay. I am sorry. I didn't know.' So she went to another table, and she was told the same thing by another resident. And then she went to a third table, and a staff person came by and said, 'Well, you can't sit there because that's where Mr. and Mrs. Smith sit.' So, she got back into the elevator and never went down to the dining room for twenty years."

This is a cautionary tale. The tragedy was her whole experience in that community, and twenty years of possible connections were lost. She took meals in her room, which is not good for her health because we're all social creatures. This could have been stopped by any one person saying, "Oh, please let me help find you a seat."

The community could have a welcome committee, which I highly recommend. With pre-planning, they could have taken an extra step so she wasn't alone on her first visit to the dining room and organized some introductions to other residents who they thought might have something in common with her.

Odd Man Out

When I was training in my very early years, we talked about setting the table and having the dining room ready, and one of the residents said to me, "I feel like the odd man out."

I said, "Why is that?"

And she said, "Well, every time I come down to the dining room, all the tables are set for couples."

She continued, "And I don't know where to sit. I don't know where to go. I am the odd man out."

I had never thought of that, and neither had the staff.

This community decided to address this by introducing a community table so people could come down and sit as a group. They found this especially helpful when a new resident was coming down to the dining room. This took some time to catch on, but residents embraced it. Those at the community table were keen to ask new residents to join them. Many communities in this post-pandemic era have developed new approaches to organizing seating in their dining rooms. Some have multiple community tables, depending on size and dining venue. This was a different kind of preparation that not only impacted new residents but also helped current residents feel they had a place at the table.

Integrating Head, Hands, And Heart

How often do you look at your dining room from the perspective of your residents and their visiting family members? If you have residents who need assistance, are you making sure to set up their place settings so they do not have to ask for assistance and feel singled out?

Having checklists, a set of best practices, and service standards for the dining experience will set your service team up for success.

What can you and your team do to put standards into practice? First things first.

Teach the importance of setting the table to meet expectations.

I am always surprised when I ask students to draw a place setting. Try it yourself. Many panic. From managers to teenagers to direct care workers. They are much more comfortable when we turn it into a group exercise, and there is a lot of conversation about how people are not dining around the table at home these days.

However, I like to stress that residents, especially the ladies, are experts and come from an era when it was good manners and etiquette on display to have the table set with everything in its place.

First, decide how you want your table and place settings arranged. In every dining venue, teach everyone how to do it right. Don't assume they know. Create pictures and post them.

If you do not have a checklist for preparing the room, tables, and serving stations, create one.

Have each team member create a list of the important dining setup tasks they do. Have them compare lists with their counterparts, with everyone contributing to the final list for each area. And if you aren't sure where to start, AI can help you create at least the start of a checklist that you can modify for your particular community. And remember—checklists need to be reviewed and updated quarterly. A checklist prepared in advance anticipates everything.

Checklists help us maintain standards and stay on track when we may feel the need to move faster or feel overwhelmed. They also help us slow down and be more confident, which can help ensure standards are met and that staff stay focused and energized during each meal service.

It can be challenging to stay engaged, especially when you are personally feeling overwhelmed, inadequate, or when there is a shortage of staff and resources. Having a standard to strive for at each meal can help keep your morale up and your energy going. You are maintaining a standard of hospitality service and working every day to achieve noble work. That alone is so much to be proud of.

It may be small acts of service to you, but to the residents, it shows the level of attention and care that you provide to each meal, each setting, and each resident. While you are a "visitor" in their home, you are also a key part of what makes this community a loving home for your residents.

Instead of looking at serving meals as an item to check off, or worse, a task that does not need any real focus, take the time to be intentional. Prepare the dining room and prepare yourself (your appearance and attitude). Look at every meal as an opportunity to showcase stellar hospitality and a belief that the residents are special because they are part of this community.

7

Consistency Elevates Service Quality

I was going in to train and introduce Kind Dining to the department heads in a continuing care community. On that day, I was scheduled to talk to Nurse Carrie, who oversees the residents in long-term care.

I was meeting her for the first time, and my first impression was that she was somewhat of a drill sergeant and not very interested in talking to me. She really didn't think that there was anything that they could improve in the way they approached serving meals.

We could see one of her employees through the window. We were in the middle of talking about the importance and value of training, and this particular employee was getting out of her car. She had her toddler on her hip, and she was in the middle of an argument with her boyfriend.

Nurse Carrie turned to me and she said, "Cindy, look what I have to work with. It's very difficult to get people to work in this job and take it seriously."

I was shocked by the conversation. And so, I asked Nurse Carrie, "Tell me a little bit about your process of serving meals. Specifically, how do you take a food order in this setting?"

She responded curtly, "We don't take orders here."

And so, I asked, "How do you ask the residents what they would like to eat?"

"We just ask them."

She didn't see the irony. How could she motivate her staff to treat people with more dignity and respect if she herself didn't have an attitude of being helpful? If she wasn't being kind, consistent, and demonstrating the values she wanted to see, why would anyone follow?

Coincidentally, the employee with a young child took the training to heart. She learned how important the dining experience was to her residents, honed her new skills, and consistently applied them to better relate to her residents and co-workers.

I checked back with her a few weeks later, and she said she enjoyed her job more. However, she was thinking of applying for a different job in this large continuing care community, to work upstairs in the independent living dining room or the housekeeping department. She took it upon herself to become more professional and advance her role in this community.

Consistency Is Key

Dining styles will differ, and the residents' abilities to eat and dine will vary, but consistency in the server's approach must be maintained throughout a community. Consistent service standards, along with an attitude of hospitality, are important for servers to demonstrate. Learning these critical foundational serving skills and techniques allows the flow of the meal to happen naturally.

In my experience, people want to do a better job. People can understand the benefits and start to take their work more seriously when they are offered an opportunity to do so. And they will want to do better.

I have yet to run into somebody who outright refuses to improve, and I have been doing training and consulting in the industry for a long time. Now, I have run into people who say, "Well, this is not for me." However, once they learn what impact the job can have, they want to do more.

Countless people simply haven't been given an opportunity to be heard and make a contribution. I believe everybody can make an impact, have a work environment where they can have an opinion, and feel listened to and heard. This is an opportunity for community executives to establish a culture of psychological safety. And staff can express their opinions without being put down or demoted for it.

This means creating an environment where you can disagree without allowing staff to become disagreeable. That's what everybody longs for. And that is exactly what I've developed in Kind Dining. By having consistent training and written service standards, all staff can understand what behaviors they are expected to exhibit and see that everyone is held to the same standard.

One Person Can Impact Many

Marla Miller, RN, BSN, PHN, IP-BC, was an amazing advocate for training and Kind Dining. She was the corporate grant coordinator for St. Francis Health Services, Morris, Minnesota. She has since passed, but her legacy lives on.

From her nursing perspective, she embraced the training, even becoming a Kind Dining instructor. Marla took it upon herself to build a team of instructors across thirteen different post-acute and assisted living communities, and from several different departments. The goal was clear: to improve residents' nutritional health and well-being by reducing unintended weight loss.

The path to this goal was to build stronger staff relationships, starting in the dining environment. There became a focus on better socialization for residents by leveraging staff education. Because Marla encouraged training and growth for so many of their staff, her organization was able to elevate the level of service and lower the unintended weight loss of residents under her watch.

Marla brought training to thirteen different communities under the St. Francis umbrella. Fourteen people were trained to be instructors. There were hundreds of students and hundreds of residents who this one individual impacted.

Some people say one person can't make a difference. Marla didn't believe that. She set out to make a difference that impacted hundreds of lives. She demonstrated the importance of consistency across all staff members, and the residents and staff benefited from holding everyone to a higher standard.

As she put it, "As a trainer, it is rewarding to see the dialogue in the room. I could see the walls of communication open up between departments, and the excitement of knowing they could all work together and bring more meaning and purpose to their work, to the lives of our residents, and to each other. On the back of the participant evaluation, I had participants write down three things they learned that they would put into practice right away. I think this is impactful as it helps staff commit to putting into action what they have learned from the Kind Dining training."

Does Your Staff Have Alzheimer's?

I was talking to a new administrator in a community where the majority of residents were Alzheimer's patients. We were discussing standards, since the kitchen staff had informed me there was a problem with not starting lunch service on time.

The administrator didn't see it as a big problem. He turned to me and said, "Our residents have Alzheimer's. They don't know if the meal is late."

My question back to him was, "Does your staff have Alzheimer's?"

What are the standards, and what are the excuses? Starting lunch consistently late impacts staff and their duties, in more than one department, not to mention disappointing the occasional family members visiting. It also implies that standards didn't really matter, because the residents wouldn't remember anyway.

If you slip here, what else are you not doing 100 percent as it should be? Are you training your staff only to follow standards because someone is watching, or are you doing things to standard every time because that is how things are done well? Are you only concentrating on reaching the minimum requirements, or are you striving for higher standards?

Integrating Head, Hands, And Heart

Service standards are not just for creating a positive environment for the residents. It also ensures the safety and well-being of the residents. We should always commit to serving the highest-quality food we can afford in a comfortable, enjoyable dining environment. If you wouldn't eat the food being served in your dining room every day, you shouldn't be serving it.

Service standards and best practices help teams focus on the dining hospitality that residents and their family members expect. Communities I go into either have no written service standards, have weak ones, or are using government regulation as their standards. Most of the time, every community has written food standards, but few have written service standards.

If you want to remain competitive and meet resident expectations consistently, you've got to do far better than the minimum.

As leaders, we need to be very clear about what excellent service looks like. Whatever customer service standards you apply to your independent dining room, they should be equally visible in each dining venue and level of care.

Service standards are the level of service we are committed to achieving under every circumstance. They should not be used to come down on people. In *The Art of Possibility: Transforming Professional and Personal Life*, Rosamund Stone Zander and Benjamin Zander focus on assuming people are capable and of making the outcome the goal.[16] Otherwise, you are "lining up with the standards against [the] students." Our job as managers and learners is to allow barriers to fall away and let "the standards maintain themselves."

Standards help to set a goal of excellence that, when communicated well, everyone understands and willingly adheres to. Standards help us look at the possibilities, and the possibilities are endless. This isn't perfectionism. This is inviting us to achieve more together.

Service standards and best practices (just as good manners and etiquette simplify mealtimes) will make your dining environment more enjoyable.

There are three key aspects of delivering great customer service in any setting that are distinctive and need to be understood separately: the personal side, the process side, and the product side of service (the three P's).

Personal refers to our human connection and interactions. Residents are the lifeblood of every community. How we behave and how we make them feel shows them how much they are valued. They want servers to be sensitive to their needs, knowledgeable, helpful, and to show they actually enjoy providing service. This includes showing courtesy, compassion, and respect, even if we are under stress.

Process refers to the actionable steps to serving. It defines the type and timing of service. What is the setup for different dining rooms or venues (wait service, action stations, mobile cart, or room service)?

The product is the quality of the food. Are we meeting the dietary needs of each resident? Is the food served at the right temperature, and is it tasty?

Now I have to almost tie my hands together in order not to go down the hospitality rabbit hole. This is because you may think that, when I say *hospitality*, it means being a waiter. Let me share with you my definition, which I want to become yours as well: *Hospitality transforms communities into civil environments.* Hospitality is an attitude and universal language to treat others as you would want to be treated first (the Golden Rule—reach out first to help someone intentionally). A civil environment naturally lifts others up and intuitively puts others before ourselves.

Through practicing the discipline of maintaining consistency, staff can own the dining experience and perform the needed skills to reduce errors, maintain health and safety protocols, and ensure an enjoyable dining experience at every meal.

This can be as simple as repeating orders correctly, bringing each course in proper sequence, not having residents wait too long for their food, serving using proper technique so that nothing spills, and being mindful each time we come to the table to see if there is anything else the residents or a co-worker may need.

By committing each meal service to following standards and processes, staff can consistently provide a pleasurable meal experience and feel proud of their work.

How good can your company get? Take this opportunity to create best practices and remove limits on yourself and your co-workers. I have provided a simple set of service standards in the resources section of the book to get you started.

8

Servers Spark Mealtime Magic

Kathy, a registered dietitian and Kind Dining instructor, worked with Molly, a newly trained food server, in the dining room. They decided to try something new with Molly. They started focusing on socialization in the dining room.

The first step was getting residents to get to know one another and making sure that everybody was happy with what they were eating. They would proactively fix any problems with the meals. They saw the impact right away. That change in their behavior reduced tensions. Family members felt more welcome and chose to visit and have meals with their relatives more often. Family members would get to know one another as well.

It changed the conversations in the dining room. In fact, one of the strangest things was that family members would still come and eat even when their relative had passed away. They enjoyed keeping up to date on their favorite servers (generally young people) and visiting friends of their loved ones. It became a community in and of itself.

Another thing they learned is that more of the staff wanted to be part of the dining magic. When they first implemented Kind Dining training, they did not include the housekeepers because they believed they didn't play a role. The housekeepers heard such great reviews of the training that they insisted on being involved.

What the leaders didn't realize was that housekeepers play a bigger role in dining than they thought. Because they are staff who go into residents' rooms to clean, they can see if there are issues that may not be considered. For example, some residents have a tendency to hoard silverware or put food in cups and take it back to their rooms. So, housekeepers could keep an eye out for missing silverware, plates, or cups and bring them back to the kitchen. That not only reduced clutter in residents' rooms but also reduced the cost of food service directors replacing items they thought were lost. The items were simply sanitized and put back where they belonged.

Soon, other ancillary staff (from recreation, nursing, or marketing) wanted to join—i.e., to be a hostess for a few meals and do this good work together. This wasn't just a paycheck for them. They wanted to make a difference in people's lives and practice what they learned in training.

That led to even more staff camaraderie across departments and happier, healthier residents. This positive socialization process again contributed to improving residents' health and well-being and lowering overall unintentional weight loss. The key was that so many other staff members were looking out for the residents and each other while magic was being made.

Don't Miss The Magic Moments—Build On Them

Remember, it's not the residents' responsibility to set the ambiance at mealtimes. Trained servers embrace their new role by connecting with residents and each other, being attentive, and taking ownership of the meal (product and service). We are teaching a new mindset along with a skill set so that as servers and supporting staff, you become the conduit to get people talking, sharing, laughing, or just enjoying the moment to be present when sharing a meal.

Those magic moments can impact not only the residents but also family members who come to spend time with them and the dining room staff. When we elevate the dining experience, everyone benefits.

Apple Pie For Dessert

A surveyor challenged me to get to know the residents in one of the communities where I was working. So, I started asking the residents what their favorite desserts were. This was triggered by my experience at False Island—getting to know just one simple thing about a person can make all the difference.

I've always started with the dessert conversation. It is amazing how people open up when they share their favorite dessert. And usually, there is a wonderful memory of family and connection surrounding that dessert.

In getting to know Mr. Anderson, I found out that apple pie was his favorite dessert. In fact, he shared with me that his mom's apple pie would earn a ribbon at the state fair every year. Now, I knew that I couldn't give him apple pie every night. What I could do was make sure that he knew that I knew apple pie was his favorite dessert. And when it was coming up on the menu, I made a point of letting him know ahead of time.

The key to building relationships with the residents is that you care because you have taken the time to get to know them: micro-moments. It wasn't about serving apple pie every night—it was about recognizing that this was his favorite dessert (and knowing his mom's ribbon-winning apple pie came with unforgettable memories for him). The importance of this type of care, with a focus on connection, is well documented in research.[17]

> The key to building relationships with the residents is that you care because you have taken the time to get to know them: micro-moments.

Building connections with people doesn't require as much time as you might think. In our communities, we see mostly the same people each day. The key is to notice them when we see them, acknowledge them, and connect, even for just a few seconds. This intentionality of connection is something that residents desire, and finding opportunities for this connection can be learned and practiced, even if staff have limited time.[18]

Where Is The Food?

I was in Vermont providing a three-day workshop. It was lunchtime and the residents, along with several family members visiting, were waiting for the meal to be served. In Vermont, it is a regulation that a licensed caregiver is present in the dining room when a meal is being served. So, they were waiting for the licensed nursing assistant (LNA) to arrive.

Time was passing, tension was rising, and still no LNA had made it to the dining room. The family members and residents were upset that the food wasn't being served. The kitchen staff was upset that they had made this effort to prepare a meal, and it was not being eaten.

However, the LNA was not the villain in this story. She was helping a resident, and that took a bit of time. She had not meant to be late—the timing was unfortunate. She either couldn't or did not think to call the kitchen to let them know, or even call another LNA to cover for her to get the meal started on time. As an observer, I noticed several LNAs having lunch in the staff room while this was unfolding.

With Kind Dining training, this group of managers and direct-care staff made several bold decisions. First, they created three committees: one for the personal side of service, one for the process side, and one for the product side. They included representatives from different departments on the committees and rotated staff every few months so they could serve on each of those committees.

This allowed them to brainstorm ways to support foodservice and caregiving staff mutually. They adjusted the staff lunch schedules and came up with the idea to have a main LNA and a backup LNA meet in the dining room. If one was tied up with other duties, there was still a second one coming in, and they could be present for the meal to be served and assist for fifteen minutes in the dining room as needed.

They also uncovered an underlying issue between this resident and that LNA. They reassigned this resident to a different caregiver with whom she got along better. This topic of better matching staff and residents became the focus of the service committee's personal side.

By focusing on the three P's, they were able to take a challenging regulation and make it magical.

Resident health and well-being is vastly improved with these conversations and staff support. And as Diana White, PhD, and Serena Hasworth, MPH, shared in their research,[19] "If relationships between residents and staff are important, then training and necessary support for staff time should be clearly prioritized and communicated."

Integrating Head, Hands, And Heart

Mealtimes are often the highlight of our day because we are human and able to converse, enjoy food, and socialize. It is a valuable part of your residents' daily quality of life, too, and should be shared as a wonderful gift to provide to someone every day.

Not all residents will want to eat in the dining room all the time. They may prefer their own solitude, and we have to respect that. However, we can make room service a great experience in its own right. When we bring in their meal, even if it is on the finest hotel wooden tray and someone sets it down with respect, if they never return, that is a problem. Something could have been missed on the tray, and the resident will feel like they are not valued.

This is especially true in a rehab facility. Take the time to knock on the door, wait for an invite to come in, smile, introduce yourself and the meal, and check the tray for anything missing. This may take a few seconds if the staff person is trained on what to do and look for. Circling back two to three minutes later to do a double-check if anything is needed is another level of caring and respect, with only a few seconds added to the engagement. We all want to be treated as people, not as tasks to complete (hence the book's title).

Room service is often overlooked as a way to make a positive lasting impression on a member from outside your senior living community.

Someone may be recuperating temporarily and, having received excellent attentive service, may become a potential permanent resident in the future.

Don't waste moments like this.

Instead of focusing on tasks to get through a dining service, think positively to leverage those moments to smile, make eye contact, and learn something about each resident. With practice, these mannerisms become natural. Always treat others with respect and dignity, and work to make their time at the table an enjoyable experience. It may surprise you how it helps you to feel better, too.

We all want to be treated as people,
not as tasks to complete (hence the book's title).

Being courteous to an older adult may mean something very different from what you feel is courtesy. Some residents may want to be addressed with their formal name (Mr. or Mrs. Smith). Other residents may insist you call them by their first name. When starting a conversation, there might be a phrase or question that can help a resident proceed into the conversation or help you transition out in order to keep serving the meal. Being aware of what helps with transitions in conversing, how to address individual residents, and expectations of formality will help show due respect.

There will be times when residents around the table may not be able to converse, but know they can hear and sense the ambiance. Always be inclusive and strive to make eye contact with each individual. If you and a co-worker are assisting residents to eat, never talk over the residents to converse with each other.

If you know a resident will want extra salad dressing with their meal or creamer for coffee, make sure you offer it even if they forget to ask. If there is a particular dessert on the menu that a resident likes, mention it to them as they sit down for the meal. Small details make magical moments, and that includes ensuring all team members communicate individual resident preferences to ensure a consistent experience.

Whether silence or a conversation is happening in the dining room, the personal skill of attending is critical. We can be curious about the person across from us and make our service more personal. When we take the time to notice someone, we communicate that we care for them. We are also able to pick up on their feelings, and we can respond more appropriately. For example, we will avoid joking with someone who seems very sad or challenging someone who seems agitated.

Your life expands when you are comfortable engaging with someone first and being in tune with their current emotional state. Yes, there will be times when we need to end a conversation. One staff member shared with me that she touches the person's arm or shoulder to show she values them before she gets back into work. Being courteous can go a long way to reassuring another person that this won't be the last time you will chat with them.

9

Emotions Fuel Authentic Connection

I did a two-day training session at a newly remodeled post-acute care community, with the head honchos in the room, from the CEO all the way down to the dishwasher. We had them all in the room together. One of the directors of nursing said, "Hey, we don't have time to pour coffee at dinner. We have other stuff we need to do."

I graciously reminded her of everyone who was in the training, and maybe we could look at this a little bit differently. We continued going through the different modules, and everyone, including this nurse, practiced pouring coffee and serving plates.

That night, she chose to test herself by pouring coffee, unbeknownst to any of the staff on duty. We came back the next day, and she told this story, "When I started pouring coffee, the staff was so appreciative of what I was doing. I was amazed." They showed her such gratitude for the ten minutes that she spent doing this that she was overwhelmed. Because of that one interaction, she said she would commit to being more involved in the serving aspect, especially when staff were short. And she did.

I've never felt that any job was beneath me in all the jobs I have ever done.

From the first day working in the nursing home, I felt I worked for the residents. They were my customers. I thought they ultimately paid my salary. So, pleasing them brought me such satisfaction. It often wasn't easy to balance all the emotions in the building, but growing into this work through observation, listening, asking questions, gaining insights, and developing new skills helped me want to give back.

I needed to understand more about how and why the system, especially around the dining environment, worked the way it did. I saw some things happening to residents and staff that needed to change, and I knew I could make a difference.

One oddity that didn't make sense to me was that jobs in "dietary" are often considered dead ends. They can be perceived as menial and often unprofessional because some require only minimal education, compared to caregiving, nursing, or "upper" management. They were traditionally paid less, and a person's position on the traditional hierarchy of the medical model mattered.

As a restaurant owner, I walked in believing the kitchen is the heart of the community and questioned why we were all not working on the same team. The moment that led me to believe that I could make a difference in how things were being done happened in that dining room.

My first thought had been that the wrong people were serving the food. In fact, the caregivers seemed to be working for a completely different organization. I knew the kitchen needed them to help it function properly. While they were working hard to serve meals, they honestly had no connection to or ownership over the quality of the food or service.

I surmised this was because they were not being taught that how we served meals mattered. This was not just in relation to meeting their customers' expectations, but also how it helped the company that hired them succeed.

So, the seed was planted in my mind that someday, I would build a training series where people who were lacking this knowledge and the interpersonal skills to pull it off could gain those insights.

Kind Dining is the result of that ambitious dream. It is a hospitality training series designed after the best elements of fine dining (service standards, best practices, consistent and ongoing training, customer-centric skills, i.e., "give them more than they expect"[20] as eloquently outlined and demonstrated by Will Guidara in his book, *Unreasonable Hospitality*). These elements are combined with the best components of culture change (honoring older adults, putting residents' needs first, respecting residents' individual rights across dining venues, and ensuring people feel at home).

The Emotional Landscape Of Senior Living

Post-acute care and senior living communities are unlike any other workplace. Here, emotions run deeper and closer to the surface than in most environments. When people live in such close proximity, sharing meals, common spaces, and daily routines, every interaction carries emotional weight. The residents we serve aren't just customers—they're people who've made our community their home, often during some of the most vulnerable periods of their lives.

Understanding this emotional intensity isn't a weakness; it's the foundation of exceptional care. When we recognize that dining interactions are deeply emotional experiences rather than simple transactions, we begin to see the actual impact of our work.

In the words of Steve Shields, from his book *In Pursuit of the Sunbeam: A Practical Guide to Transformation from Institution to Household*, "We must begin at home to create home. When we, as long-term care leaders, begin changing the culture of nursing homes in our own communities, everybody and everything else will follow suit."[21]

Mastering Communication Through Difficult Moments

When mistakes happen—and they will—our response defines the relationship. The ability to listen actively, truly seeing situations from our residents' perspectives, or our co-workers', transforms a potential conflict into an opportunity for deeper connection. A sincere apology isn't just words; it's an acknowledgment of someone's experience and feelings. Learning to de-escalate emotional tensions requires us to step outside our own defensive reactions and meet people where they are emotionally.

This skill extends beyond crisis management. Every day, we have opportunities to practice these communication tools, building stronger relationships with each interaction.

Having and sharing even basic feelings of anger, upset, happiness, or fear at various points in a day or week, while living and working in such close proximity as in a care community, are all part of being alive and building trust. When we create an environment where emotions can be expressed safely, we're not just providing good customer service—we're nurturing the human spirit with an attitude of hospitality.

Building Trust Through Vulnerability

Emotional authenticity builds deeper connections than any perfectly executed procedure ever could. When residents see that we're real people who understand their struggles, fears, and joys, trust develops naturally. These dining moments become opportunities for genuine human connection, where a simple conversation over coffee can transform someone's entire day.

The wide range of emotions experienced in our communities isn't something to be managed or contained—it's something to be acknowledged, validated, and honored as part of the human experience.

Learn While You Earn

Professional composure doesn't mean becoming emotionally numb. It means developing the skills to stay present and caring even when situations become challenging. This requires ongoing support, training, and most importantly, the recognition that emotional resilience is a skill that can be developed and strengthened over time.

Staff learning emotional self-management techniques isn't just beneficial for our residents—it's essential for our own well-being in this emotionally demanding work.

Growing Together Through Learning

The most successful care communities are those that embrace continuous learning and emotional intelligence skills. This means encouraging personal reflective practices that help staff understand their own emotional responses and creating opportunities to learn from every experience.

Training focused on emotional intelligence isn't separate from technical skills—it enhances every aspect of care delivery. When staff members can recognize emotional cues, respond with empathy, and manage their own reactions effectively, the entire community benefits.

These skills develop over time through practice, reflection, and ongoing support from leadership and colleagues. To better ourselves, we must look at how we are seen from others' viewpoints. Self-awareness is the secret ingredient for personal growth.

Emotional well-being isn't an add-on to physical care—it's integral to overall resident health and satisfaction. When we teach the emotional skills needed (or missing) in our dining service protocols, we're acknowledging the whole person, not just their physical needs.

Beyond The Physical Act Of Service

Training staff to see beyond the physical act of serving food to the emotional experience of dining changes everything. Suddenly, the way we present a meal, the tone of our voice, and the attention we pay to preferences and concerns all become part of the care we provide. This holistic approach recognizes that nourishing someone involves much more than delivering nutrients through food. It's nourishing a person's soul when we show care through the love and unfailing generosity we show.

The work of emotional intelligence in senior living and post-acute care isn't easy, but it's the work that transforms good care into exceptional care. It's what turns a dining service into a community experience, and what makes the difference between a place where people live and a place where people truly feel at home.

Every post-acute and senior living community can transform its dining experiences from mere meal services to meaningful, emotionally supportive interactions that enhance residents' quality of life and overall well-being.

In a speech, Margaret Tyson, dean of the School of Nursing, University of Virginia, famously said that people don't care how much you know until they know how much you care. When a Kind Dining trainer was teaching a class, the staff came up with a great idea on how to interact better and to get to know the residents and their co-workers.

Some of the younger staff shared that on their personal name tags, in big print, they could put their favorite sports team or their favorite hobby. The residents could look at their name, and they would have something to start a conversation. Starting up small talk is a learned skill that oftentimes needs to be taught to take hold. This allowed the younger staff members to practice the art of conversation and get to know fellow staffers and the residents better. It was a win-win.

Requesting Three Hot Fudge Sundaes

One of the residents at a senior living community asked if she could buy two extra sundaes for the upcoming weekend. Her grandkids were coming to visit, and even though she could not "take them out," she wanted to do something special and create a memory and maybe even a ritual of hot fudge sundaes with Grandma.

It wasn't the food that was the request; it was the creation of a beautiful memory her grandchildren would have long after she was gone. I bet you won't look at a hot fudge sundae the same way again.

Integrating Head, Hands, And Heart

The quality of life for residents and the quality of work for staff are greatly impacted by the dining experience. Having a sense of belonging and connection is imperative for residents who may feel isolated or no longer have the freedom they once had.

Did you know that many residents see staff more often than they see their own family members?[22] What are you doing in your daily work to pick up on the emotional state of your residents? If a resident in your community is upset, do you try to understand, be patient, and get someone who can help, or do you dismiss their concerns?

Emotions are not the enemy—they allow us to share grievances and be heard. Realizing your residents will experience both positive and negative emotions you may not fully understand, yet knowing how to respond to them, can build stronger connections and more powerful relationships.

As a food service director, one needs very broad shoulders. I learned that more often than not, when a resident was complaining about the food, the real disappointment was that their children canceled coming for lunch, a friend passed away, or they had a medication change.

Many residents in your community are experiencing loss of loved ones and the fear of their own mortality. Be present, be empathetic, be compassionate.

10

Safety Guards Every Plate

In one of my first career assignments in a residential healthcare setting, I was observing the breakfast service. There was a flutter of activity—surveyors were coming into the building.

It was my first time talking with a surveyor. I felt that it wouldn't be a problem or a challenge for me because the kitchen was clean, sanitized, and organized. I thought that was my biggest responsibility as the kitchen manager, but what Arlene, the surveyor, asked me was why Mr. Anderson was on that particular diet.

Of course, I told her it was because the nurse says so, and they give you this little card with the diet order on it. And Arlene looked me right in the eye and she said, "That's not a good enough answer. You need to know Mr. Anderson well enough to answer that question yourself." Then she added, "You need to be another set of eyes and ears to protect the resident."

Food Safety First With Your Residents

Older adults are more at risk of contracting a foodborne illness. This reality hit me hard early in my career when I witnessed firsthand how quickly a minor oversight could escalate into a serious health crisis for our most vulnerable residents. It changed my entire outlook on what we do in food services and dining operations—working with this age group and vulnerable population. We're not just serving meals; we're serving as guardians of health for people who depend on us completely.

The truth about our aging residents is both humbling and sobering. Their immune systems, weakened by age and often compromised by medications and chronic conditions, cannot fight off foodborne pathogens the way younger, healthier people can. What might cause a day or two of discomfort for someone in their thirties could land one of our residents in the hospital or worse.

There are no minor cases of food poisoning for this age group. The complications can be severe—dehydration, kidney problems, even life-threatening infections. When we understand that food safety isn't just a protocol but a critical health protection measure, every action we take in the kitchen and dining rooms carries new weight and meaning.

For our purposes in this book, food safety awareness and food-borne illness prevention will focus on front-of-house service, not back-of-house service (the kitchen).

The Life-Or-Death Reality

This isn't meant to scare anyone, but rather to help us understand the profound responsibility we carry. This knowledge should inform every decision we make, every procedure we follow, and every moment of training we provide to our staff.

Often, our food servers come to us with good intentions but little to no professional food safety experience. They're eager to help, ready to learn, but they don't yet understand the invisible dangers that can lurk in seemingly innocent situations. I see this most often with young new hires, who are serving meals for the very first time. They often receive limited to no professional training.

No one is born knowing the basics of food safety and how, as servers, they might contribute to or prevent a foodborne illness outbreak. And because many communities use an all-hands dining approach, which I support, staff serving meals often work in departments that are not considered part of the nutrition and food service department, e.g., recreation, wellness, speech therapy, nursing and caregiving, marketing, and housekeeping. And many do not receive food safety training. This is where systematic, thorough training becomes not just helpful, but essential. At the very least, each employee serving food and beverages in any dining venue must have a food handler's card.

Creating Learning That Sticks

People learn differently—some need to see it, others need to do it, and many need to read about it later to reinforce what they've learned. Effective food safety training uses all these approaches. Visual guides posted in work areas, hands-on practice under supervision, written materials to review, and, most importantly, the opportunity to ask questions without feeling foolish.

I've learned that competency verification isn't about testing people to see if they fail—it's about ensuring they have the confidence and knowledge to succeed. When someone can demonstrate proper handwashing technique, explain why we don't touch ready-to-eat foods with our bare hands, or identify when something needs to be discarded, they're not just following rules—they're protecting lives.

Safety in senior living and post-acute care isn't complicated, but it is critical. The basics—proper handwashing, understanding temperature danger zones, preventing cross-contamination, maintaining clean, sanitized, and disinfected work surfaces, and paying attention to our own personal health and hygiene—aren't just suggestions. They're the foundation of everything we do.

Making It Simple And Clear

Step-by-step protocols work because they remove guesswork. When staff members have clear, visual guides they can reference quickly, they're more likely to follow proper procedures consistently. I've found that checklists become second nature when they're used regularly and when staff understand not just what to do, but why it matters.

The goal isn't to create robots who follow procedures blindly, but to build understanding so deep that safe practices become instinctive.

One of the most important things we can teach our staff is how easy it is to accidentally spread contamination. It's not about carelessness or bad intentions; it's about understanding how pathogens move and multiply in ways we can't see.

The Invisible Threats

A server touches their hair and then handles a dinner roll. Someone wipes down a table with disinfectant and then carries clean plates without washing their hands. A well-meaning staff member tastes food with a spoon and then uses that same spoon to serve. These aren't acts of negligence—they're normal human behaviors that become dangerous in a food service environment.

When we help staff understand these risks, we're not making them paranoid—we're making them aware. Knowledge removes the mystery and helps people make better choices instinctively.

The best food safety programs aren't built on fear or punishment—they're built on understanding, support, and shared responsibility. When everyone, from the dishwasher to the registered dietitian to the resident care manager, sees themselves as part of the safety team, remarkable things happen.

Positive Reinforcement Works

I've seen the difference it makes when we celebrate excellent safety practices rather than only addressing problems. When we acknowledge someone for consistently following proper procedures, share success stories, and make food safety heroes visible, we create an environment where people want to do the right thing.

Regular audits shouldn't feel like inspections designed to catch people doing wrong—they should feel like opportunities to recognize good work and identify areas where we can provide better support or training.

Perhaps the most powerful way to build commitment to food safety is to help staff understand the human impact of their actions. When they realize that Mrs. Johnson in room 204, who reminds them of their own grandmother, could become seriously ill from a moment of inattention, food safety becomes personal. *Something as simple as assigning kitchen staff to get to know the residents can help with making safety a habit.*

Connecting Care To Safety

Food safety is an expression of respect and compassion. When we handle food safely, we're saying to our residents, "You matter. Your health matters. You deserve to feel confident that every meal we serve you has been prepared and delivered with your well-being as our top priority."

This connection between safety and caring helps new servers understand that they're not just learning procedures—they're learning how to express love, respect, and professionalism through their work.

New servers often feel overwhelmed by everything they need to learn. Food safety training should build confidence, not create anxiety. When we provide thorough, supportive training that allows people to practice and ask questions, we're setting them up for success.

Supporting Success

I've found that people rise to meet expectations when those expectations are clear and when they feel supported in meeting them. Safety training that includes mentorship, ongoing check-ins, and opportunities to ask questions helps new staff members develop not just knowledge but confidence in their ability to protect the people they serve.

Safety isn't separate from resident care—it's integral to it. When we integrate safety education into our broader understanding of resident wellness, we help staff see how every aspect of their work contributes to the quality of life for the people we serve.

Beyond Compliance

The goal isn't just to pass health department inspections or avoid citations—it's to create an environment where residents can trust completely that every meal they receive has been handled with the utmost care and attention to their safety.

This holistic perspective helps staff understand that they're not just following safety rules—they're participating in a comprehensive approach to resident care that values safety, dignity, and well-being equally.

The most successful senior living and post-acute care communities are those where every staff member, regardless of their specific role, sees themselves as a guardian of resident health. The housekeeper who properly sanitizes dining room tables, the recreation director who ensures snacks are stored safely, the maintenance worker who keeps equipment running properly—everyone plays a role.

Shared Responsibility

When we build a culture where safety is taught universally and where it is everyone's responsibility, where questions are welcomed, where continuous learning is expected, and where the well-being of our residents drives every decision, we create an environment where foodborne illness outbreaks and other safety issues become virtually impossible.

This isn't about perfection—it's about commitment, knowledge, and the understanding that in senior living, safety isn't just good business practice. It's a sacred trust between us and the vulnerable people who have chosen to make our community their home. And this is also about being there for one another to ensure that a resident is well looked after, whether that means feeling mentally, physically, or emotionally secure.

The *Journal of Food Protection* estimates that, aggregated across all US states, the average national cost of foodborne illnesses in 2015 was $55.5 billion.[23] That number most likely has gone up.

Protecting our residents through proper safety practices requires vigilance, knowledge, and compassion. But when we get it right, we're doing more than preventing illness—we're providing the foundation that allows our residents, their family members, guests, and staff to enjoy their meals with confidence, dignity, and peace of mind.

Melba Goes To The Doctor

One of the things I learned in doing my research is that residents are getting to know each other as family. I never really understood this as an employee working in a building. They really do watch out for each other.

I often tell the story in training—if Melba goes to the doctor at nine in the morning and she's not back by noon, everybody wants to know where she is. I realized they were not just nosy; residents are keeping track of each other. When I, as an employee, would come and go, I wasn't often privy to the conversations the residents have every day.

I have learned that many employees, especially those new to working in this environment, don't realize how important these connections can be. New hires don't come into this job knowing that residents see them more often than they do their own family members. Many do count on your staff as being in that tight, familiar relationship.

There is an adage you may know, "It takes a village," and residents notice when things are out of joint. They can oftentimes be each other's safety net. Staff can be an additional net as well and step in when safety is at stake.

Integrating Head, Hands, And Heart

Older adults are at higher risk for foodborne illness due to weakened immune systems, medications, and chronic conditions. Safety should not be a rule-following exercise but a critical health protection mission where every procedure directly impacts resident well-being.

Training on safety concepts, creating step-by-step protocols, and conducting supportive assessments can build confidence, encourage constructive feedback, and foster positive reinforcement to strengthen team-wide food safety practices.

When issues arise, staff can develop the ability to investigate problems constructively, create effective corrective action plans, and build systems that encourage transparency. These skills emphasize collaboration and continuous improvement rather than punishment-based approaches.

By moving from task-oriented to person-centered interactions, food safety becomes an expression of care and respect for residents and the company that hired us, rather than just a series of tasks to complete. Staff can begin to connect their actions to the people they serve, creating an emotional investment in doing things right.

Staff can now move from reactive to proactive, thus developing the ability to anticipate and prevent problems before they occur rather than just responding to issues. This creates natural leaders who continuously look for ways to strengthen food safety practices.

11

Empowerment Transforms Dining Culture

If we truly aspire to improve dining hospitality and the community culture in which our aging adults live, we must take a serious look at how we involve the residents and staff in decision-making. Our staff serving meals are the resource for continued positive change as we value, train, listen to, and empower them to provide better care.

One of my colleagues learned this lesson the hard way while working in a senior living community. They had implemented a new menu system that looked perfect on paper—nutritionally balanced, cost-effective, and efficient to prepare. But within a week, the complaints started rolling in. Residents weren't eating. The staff were frustrated. The beautiful plan was failing miserably because they had forgotten to ask the most important question: What do the people who actually live and work here like to eat and want to see on the menus we serve?

I heard this quote from Joseph Carlin, RD, LD at my first nutrition conference in 1995: "Food must be nutritious, culturally relevant, and served with artistry, skill, and love." These words are still applicable today.

Our best intentions mean nothing if they don't reflect the voices of the people most affected by our decisions. Real change happens when we stop talking and start listening and doing.

The shift from traditional top-down management to truly collaborative decision-making requires us to fundamentally rethink who holds the power in our communities. Our residents aren't customers in the traditional sense—they're neighbors, community members, and the reason we exist. Yet too often, we make decisions about their daily experiences without asking for their input until after problems arise.

From Recipients To Partners

Here is a tip: If you're going to surprise an elderly person, you need to tell them first. To reduce resident resistance, communicate ahead of time. Let them know you're thinking of making changes in the dining program. Bring your initiatives to the resident council and food committee and ask for their help. Invite them to the focus group meetings. Get resident buy-in before you make any changes.

I've seen communities transform when they begin treating residents as active participants rather than passive recipients of care. Mrs. Patterson, who ran a restaurant for thirty years before moving into our community, had insights about meal presentation that our trained chefs had never considered. Mr. Rodriguez knew exactly why the dining room felt cold and unwelcoming—and he had practical suggestions for fixing it. These weren't complaints; they were solutions waiting to be heard.

Creating meaningful opportunities for resident input requires more than suggestion boxes that rarely get checked. It means establishing systematic ways to gather feedback, implementing changes based on that feedback, and then reporting back to residents about what happened as a result of their suggestions. When residents see that their voices lead to real changes, they become invested partners in making the community better for everyone.

Food service servers and ancillary staff serving meals, primarily caregivers, see almost everything. They know which residents are struggling with appetite, who's feeling lonely, who lights up when someone remembers they prefer their coffee black. They witness the small interactions that can make or break someone's day. Yet in many communities, these invaluable team members who are managing the dining experience are treated as someone who won't benefit from consistent professional training, rather than the key strategic partners they actually are.

Building Pathways For Growth: Encourage Life-Long Learning

When we invest in comprehensive professional development for any staff person serving meals, we're not just improving their skills—we're showing them that their work matters and their growth matters to management. Training curricula that go beyond technical skills to include hospitality, cultural sensitivity, and emotional intelligence create staff members who can connect with residents and their co-workers on multiple levels.

I've watched dishwashers become dining room supervisors, servers become activity directors, and food prep workers become certified dietary managers—but only in communities that created pathways for advancement and supported their staff's professional growth. When people see a future for themselves in senior living or post-acute care, they bring passion and commitment that can't be taught or mandated.

Meaningful engagement about change requires multiple avenues for input because people communicate differently.

From a leadership perspective, building a winning team hinges on two things:

1. How we manage conflict and create connections that improve livability and sense of community.
2. How we help our staff learn a universal language (hospitality) that creates a home/common purpose/sense of belonging.

Meaningful engagement about change requires multiple avenues for input because people communicate differently.

But as people are promoted within dining departments (and this might be said for most departments), they are not necessarily being taught leadership skills around finding a sense of purpose, getting along better, and creating a positive team dynamic, especially across departments.

Change can't happen overnight; it will require staff changing some behaviors. There will be staff resistance.

It's important to help everyone embrace change rather than fear it. The fear I run into most is people being rocked out of their comfort zone because of a lack of communication about upcoming changes and how they will affect them.

Some fail to see the connection between their job and the value of serving a meal. Have you met care partners who say, "Change just means more work," or "I wasn't hired to be a waitress"? My response would be: Are you the one carrying the plate? If so, then your role has changed in this moment, and we need you to step into it.

Staff turnover is also a major challenge in communities. Turnover among caregiving staff creates problems with service continuity and broken relationships in dining.

It's similar to when you've built a relationship with your favorite server in a restaurant that you've been patronizing for years. You're what they call a regular, and they know you have six grandkids and you're a decaf coffee drinker, but then someone new comes along and gives you regular coffee.

It's *that* kind of loss of service and of losing something you *thought* was special (an enjoyable personal connection, and a *smile* you can count on) that is gone. This recurring sense of loss can and does make some people wary, hesitant, or distrustful of reaching out again.

While you can't eliminate staff turnover or job losses, you can minimize the damage by training all community staff serving in your dining venues, especially in room service, to the same service standards. It's important to communicate about this topic while considering people's sensitivity; turnover doesn't need to automatically result in breaking core relationships with the company, especially when other employees know how to fill that void. This is especially a sensitive topic with family members.

Some residents feel comfortable speaking up in group settings; others prefer written feedback or one-on-one conversations. Some staff members will share ideas freely in team meetings; others need private conversations to feel safe expressing their thoughts.

It pays to learn more about the individual people you hire, which we'll address in part III.

What Is It That Your Staff Is Learning?

Janelle Wallace, an education manager, brings a background in nursing and instructional design to staff education at a large Canadian healthcare organization where she works. Her training covers all staff, from the C-suite to volunteers.

She shared, "When I am looking at how to leverage the investment of training, I want to know how we can make this a consistent practice for all staff and not just a select group of people. And we use the training to review and modify policies so that we are always increasing our standards and quality."

In providing training options to leadership, Janelle recognizes that cost is always a primary consideration.

"There is not just the cost of the training itself. There is taking frontline workers off their shifts and bringing in temporary coverage so they can complete the training without interruption. But the bigger cost is, if leadership chooses not to do training, how is our community being perceived? What do people say about the care we provide?"

By having leadership not only understand the impact of the training but also take the training, they can share that common language and the ideas being taught.

"Strong leaders want to know what their staff is learning and learn those new skills as well."

And to see the full impact of training, leadership needs to fully commit to the process, including having all staff complete the training within a set time window.

"If you want to see the outcomes realized, all staff need to take the training and take it together so they can practice with each other what they have learned."

Building Trust Through Transparency

The most effective feedback systems I've seen include regular dining experience surveys, resident and staff advisory forums, and informal mechanisms that capture spontaneous insights. But the key isn't just gathering input—it's creating transparent processes that show how suggestions are considered, which ones are implemented, and why some ideas aren't feasible.

When people see that their input leads to tangible changes, they become more engaged. When a staff member's suggestion to use correct portion scoop sizes reduces food waste, or when someone changes a bad habit of pre-pouring juice at breakfast to speed service and instead pours as the residents order, that person becomes a champion for continuous improvement. When a resident's feedback about the dining room atmosphere results in new lighting and music, other residents start speaking up with their own ideas.

Real cultural transformation happens when we stop seeing dining as just a nutritional service and start recognizing it as a holistic social and emotional experience, in every dining venue. This means challenging traditional institutional dining models that prioritize efficiency over humanity and creating environments that feel more like home and community.

The most impactful training programs I've implemented address not just customer service, but also culture change, cultural sensitivity, emotional intelligence, and communication techniques. When staff understand not just how to serve food, but how to connect with the people they're serving, everything changes.

Learning From Each Other

Mentorship and peer learning opportunities create natural knowledge transfer and build strong team relationships. When experienced staff members share not just technical skills but also insights about connecting with individual residents, new team members develop confidence and competence more quickly. These relationships also create support systems that help staff navigate the emotional challenges of working with our most vulnerable populations.

Ongoing education and skill development must become part of everyone's professional journey, not just an initial orientation requirement. When learning becomes part of the culture, people stay engaged, grow in their roles, and contribute to continuous improvement.

The best innovations in senior living and post-acute care dining come from the people closest to the work—the staff who see daily challenges and the residents who experience them. Creating mechanisms to pilot and implement innovative dining approaches means being open to ideas that might seem unconventional but could dramatically improve the resident experience.

In an article in *Senior Living Foresight*,[24] Jack Cumming talks about how the communal dining room experience is not the only way residents are able to dine and connect. Dining in a noisy environment may be difficult or distracting. By allowing residents to determine how they wish to dine, staff can sometimes gain insights into new issues (hearing loss, feelings of isolation, memory issues) that may be subtle enough to be missed otherwise.

Flexibility And Personalization

Technology can support more personalized dining experiences, but only when it's implemented thoughtfully with input from the people who will use it. Flexible dining models that adapt to resident preferences—whether that means different meal times, dining in various locations, or choosing from customizable menu options—require staff who understand both residents' needs and expectations, and the operational realities in their community.

I've seen communities successfully implement everything from made-to-order breakfast stations to small, intimate household dining table services, but only when the changes were developed collaboratively with resident and staff input. Jack Cumming, in the article mentioned above, discusses wanting to-go meals in the senior living community he lives in, which could add flexibility to dining options. However, he acknowledges pushback on this idea if a provider views this in the same category as room service (an added cost).

Community Building Through Meals

Some of the most powerful community-building moments I've witnessed have happened in the dining rooms. Residents can share stories about their own joy of cooking, or willingness to give it up happily; staff members can be curious and learn about different cultural traditions; families can join their loved ones for special meals, even to pop in to visit and have a cup of tea together. These interactions create the social fabric that makes a place become a home. And the most successful communities teach staff to be present in the moment with intentional focus as they do their noble work.

However, it is important to state that a community can be built where two or more people are gathered. Whatever customer service and hospitality are provided in the independent dining room need to be offered to residents in assisted living, residential, and memory care dining experiences as well. What I mean by this is the same quality of food served, along with the conviviality, kindness, and respect. These are gifts that we can give all residents and staff, feeding bodies and souls.

Whatever customer service and hospitality are provided in the independent dining room need to be offered to residents in assisted living, residential, and memory care dining experiences as well.

Celebrating Success Together

The most effective communities I've worked with celebrate successful improvements and innovations together. When a resident's suggestion leads to a popular new menu item, that person is recognized. When a staff member's process improvement makes service more efficient, that achievement is shared. These celebrations reinforce that everyone's contributions matter and encourage continued engagement.

Building trust through consistent, honest communication means acknowledging when suggestions can't be implemented and explaining why, sharing both successes and challenges, and maintaining transparency about decision-making processes.

The ultimate goal is creating dining environments that honor the dignity, preferences, and individual stories of residents while supporting staff in delivering exceptional, compassionate care. This isn't achieved through policies or procedures alone—it happens when we truly listen to the voices of the people whose lives are most affected by our decisions and empower them to be partners in creating positive change.

When residents feel heard and valued, when staff feel empowered and supported, and when leadership demonstrates genuine commitment to collaborative improvement, dining becomes more than a service. It becomes the heart of a community where people truly want to live and work.

The ultimate goal is to create dining environments at all levels of care in every organization in every dining venue that exceed residents' expectations and honor their dignity, preferences, and individual stories. People are not born knowing how to serve and treat others with kindness, love, and generosity as they give care in the dining room.

The Hamburger And The Enchilada

I was conducting an observation in a residential care community. The trays for the assisted living dining room all came up on the big cart, and the server was handing everybody out their plates. The staff member handed Bob an enchilada. And she kept delivering the other plates, even though Bob said, "I didn't order the enchilada; I ordered the hamburger."

She ignored him and went about serving. Of course, he got louder, saying, "I need a hamburger."

I said, "I'd be happy to run down to the kitchen and get Bob a burger."

The caregiver said to me, "He probably forgot that he really did order the enchilada."

I asked her, "How do you know that is what happened?"

She got a little defensive and said, "Well, the gal will be right up with the order tickets."

Turns out, Bob ordered the hamburger, and somebody in the kitchen made an error. Unfortunately, there were no more hamburgers left.

The lady across the table from Bob said, "Bob, your enchilada looks really good. Would you like to have my hamburger?"

The whole table waited for Bob to get the correct food before they started eating, and they ended up troubleshooting to get Bob the meal he actually ordered. It was a clever solution. Yes, there was a temporary fix at this meal, and you can imagine this interaction dominated the conversation for more than one meal. It also revealed a more systemic issue that we'll address in part III.

Community: Unifying Around A Common Cause Makes The Difference

One of the communities that embraced Kind Dining training, with the goal of creating a restaurant-style dining experience, shared that once their initial staff of sixty were trained, they collectively started focusing on socialization in their dining rooms, which led to higher resident dining satisfaction scores, higher staff satisfaction scores, and lower unintentional weight loss. This was only one piece of their success story.

Another piece was that this group of trainees came from all departments (including department heads from nursing, marketing, foodservice, and recreation; lead cooks; registered dietitians; certified nurse aides; recreation assistants; and newly hired teenagers). As they began to cross-train, applying new hospitality, customer service, and food serving skills, they got to know one another.

As they got to know one another, previous silos of department distinctions began to melt away. As they focused on aligned goals, they believed this work was collectively important. They took on positions such as serving as a host or hostess at lunch and politely greeting family members or introducing residents to their tablemates so they would talk with one another.

They also made sure that everybody was happy with what they were eating or quickly fixed any issues with the meals. Another big benefit of that simple change in ambiance was that more family members would visit and have meals with residents.

Other departments wanted to be a part of this experience as well. It wasn't just a paycheck. They wanted to make a difference in these people's lives and wanted the training to do so.

There was natural buy-in within the staff to contribute to the civility of the community and the experience given. When it comes to your organization, do your coworkers feel they are in this together and that they belong to a higher purpose? Do they understand the purpose of moving to a hospitality mindset with a servant's heart?

What can hospitality accomplish? When you lead with person-centered hospitality, as Kind Dining does, you are teaching civility. Kind Dining hospitality creates community—not only between servers and residents, but also among all departments. Because hospitality is at the heart and soul of my definition of community, community is defined as belonging to the group. Community is the sum of all the residents' relationships: with one another, with you as a server, with staff, and with their families.

Once you have training like Kind Dining in place, people in your company will naturally act in ways that support your residents' success, your company's success, and their own personal and professional growth.

As a community leader, your direction, support, and coaching are essential and welcome. Alignment of the mission, vision, and values sets the stage for success in every interaction within that community.

Integrating Head, Hands, And Heart

There are systematic approaches for gathering meaningful feedback from both residents and staff. This includes surveys, resident council feedback, and informal mechanisms, like suggestion boxes. It is essential to create transparent processes that show how suggestions are evaluated and implemented, along with professional development strategies that build pathways for staff advancement.

Our systems need to update as the environment does. Reviewing standard operating procedures (SOPs) for your dining department can provide vital feedback. Developing a better workflow, updating checklists, or even reviewing someone's responsibilities allows for a fluidity that keeps things running smoothly.

I was working with a large health care group in Missouri and had just taught the LEARN model (listen, empathize, ask questions, restate, and new behavior). In this discussion, I explained that nothing changes if nobody makes a change. Ultimately, it is the manager's job to get anyone who isn't getting along to get along.

It was the third day, and one of the assisted living food service managers came up to me and said, "I practiced what you talked about. I had two employees who wouldn't get along. All they did was fight and cause problems. I brought them into my office and said we were not leaving until we had worked this out because it was causing so much turmoil, and we could not continue. This is because it isn't about us, it is about the residents and their success in this community."

She hadn't realized before this moment how much the conflict between these two people prevented everyone else from doing their job well.

She finished by saying, "It worked because you gave me the strength to be a good leader and take action."

She just needed someone in her corner.

Staff must always see residents as active community partners rather than passive care recipients, unable to absorb everything going on around them. Residents are rooting for staff to be on their best behavior so they can lavish praise. Their expertise and life experience dining out qualify them to judge good and bad behavior. Few want to be a burden to staff, and most go out of their way not to complain about poor service or staff conflicts. They don't want to get the staff into trouble.

Residents are wonderful resources (and motivators) for improvement. All staff serving meals must be treated as strategic partners and receive professional training aligned with your company's mission, values, and goals.

They then possess crucial insights about resident needs and help to diffuse negative community dynamics. Leadership in communities must move beyond seeing staff who serve meals, from every department, as mere order-takers or task-completers and appreciate their role as key contributors to resident well-being, their own personal and professional success in this community, and the success of the whole community.

PART III

Invitation For Leadership: Getting Back To Basics

*"Individual commitment to a group effort—
that is what makes a team work, a company work,
a society work, a civilization work."*
Vince Lombardi

Vince Lombardi talked to his team about how they had lost their intention and focus. And he went back to basics, starting with the introduction of the football. This can also happen with staff at your community. The focus must always be on making the experience the best for the resident.

We may not be able to prevent our residents from aging, feeling pain, or having a loss. Where we can easily make an impact is around the table at every meal, and by creating a sense of belonging.

It's worth repeating that mealtimes are the highlight of your residents' day. And it needs to be taken more seriously post-pandemic. I can't say this often enough; it's the one element in your offerings that your customers universally value. And it is the one differentiator that can be entirely under your control. So, the dining experience is more than just a feel-good for the community. It's your best marketing asset.

Senior living communities that survived COVID are having to continue to rethink and reinvent much of their foodservice and dining operations as costs continue to rise. With the rising costs of operations,[25] food being one of them, encouraging residents to eat together in the dining room provides cost savings and a healthy social aspect of community living that can combat the current epidemic of loneliness and isolation that we are facing.

So, the dining experience is more than just a feel-good for the community. It's your best marketing asset.

As previously mentioned, socializing in the dining room, when done right, has a number of health benefits, like reducing unintended weight loss in residents. It also reduces the cost of food service delivery[26] in room service and contributes to residents' happiness with where they live. While some residents may prefer to eat in their room, the majority will see a tangible benefit. Many things can go right in this situation, and some things can go wrong. And there is no cost to share kindness.

"My mother's nursing home is a zombie feeding station." That sentence was in a letter I received from a daughter about the nursing home her mom was living in. She wrote me this letter because she knew I was a Kind Dining trainer and wanted something to be done. I kept in contact with her as we worked with that community. Just reaching out to her helped her envision how this might be fixed.

How do you think this impression impacted referrals and the bottom line of that community? Somebody with a positive experience might tell four people, someone with a negative experience might tell sixteen people. Marriott, in addition to hotels and restaurants, runs long-term care homes. They have done internal studies that showed the most loyal customers and advocates are people who had a problem that was fixed.

How often do you physically listen to what residents are saying about the food in your dining room? How many times do residents have to say that the brussels sprouts or vegetables in general are always soggy (yes, this still happens) before there is a fix?

Do you eat in your dining room? Are you proud that the quality of the meal is so good that you offer a free meal to a visiting family member? I have had family members complain that it's frustrating to see no improvement in food quality, and that the staff will commiserate with them and chalk it up to just being nursing home food.

The most savvy leaders in this industry[27] don't let this happen—they own and correct recurring issues in the kitchen and understand the need to hire for intention and train for retention. They also understand what their staff need to *know* in order to perform well, what they need to *do* in order to succeed, and what they need to *value* in order to positively impact the organization.

As Quint Studer has shared,[28] the professional training provided for your employees should be considered an investment, not an expense. That means there is a clear return on the efforts put into your employees to teach them how best to support your company's success.

Happy Diners Make Happy Residents

Audrey Morgan, NDTR, LDT, has been working as a food service director in senior care homes for twenty-six years. Her focus has been on community service and leadership. She shares this wisdom, "You first have to understand what resources are available and then figure out the best way to use those resources. No one is asking for millions of dollars to be spent. But, by looking for the intersection of community and connection, and using training to build those skills, you will be amazed at what your staff can accomplish to positively impact residents."

Residents who feel they can be a part of the culture change get inspired to also make changes. They will take the time to get ready for a meal, including putting on makeup and jewelry. They are more agreeable and will actively get ready, as they see it as an experience to go out. They also become more tolerant of mistakes, like misplacing one of their blouses in the laundry. Everyone benefits when a new mindset is embraced.

That change can come from unexpected places. A resident reached out to me after finding a flyer about Kind Dining training in her senior living community. She called and asked me if she could purchase thirty of my Be Kind heart pins because she wanted to extend a kindness to the kitchen and staff members serving meals there. Of course, I sent the pins free of charge, and she sent me a lovely thank-you note. You never know how residents will show up to be part of the culture change until you give them the opportunity to do so.

The four areas where leadership can make the most impact and see the greatest ROI are setting service standards, hiring well, continual training, and coaching to reinforce good behaviors. Each of these provides a foundational element to putting learning insights into practice and seeing your investment bring long-lasting dividends.

12

Setting Service Standards: Vision, Mission, Values

One of Frederick Chopin's most famous quotes[29] is that simplicity is the highest goal. It can also be the most challenging of goals to achieve, because we still have to choose it. And it can oftentimes be overlooked.

Senior living dining operations face hard challenges, balancing individualized satisfaction with efficiency (balancing budgets) while maintaining high levels of quality and safety.

It's been my experience, and I don't mean to judge, that when some executives think about budgets and need to reduce expenses, there is an impulse to cut the foodservice operation budget and spend less money on food, service, and labor without thinking about how this affects the dining experience and resident satisfaction.

To stay competitive in this new era, community leaders can't afford to take this short-term approach, because that's not going to solve their problem in the long run. If this is a chronic issue, it will result in poor-quality food, with residents discouraged from eating and staff embarrassed by the food offered. Even family members chime in with horror stories about your soggy and cold vegetables. Some will just move their family members out.

We've talked about how *you must protect the integrity of your dining service operation* to keep resident satisfaction scores high because it directly affects your occupancy rate. To do that, you need a better balance between efficiency, quality, and resident satisfaction. So maybe we need to start taking a more holistic approach: What if there's more to life than the budget? What if you could actually do more with less if everyone were working toward the same goals?

Food must be nutritious, culturally relevant, and served with artistry, skill, and love. And that is why serving has to be a team effort across departments. Communities have to serve the best food they can afford, but everyone has to support the food that is offered. You can improve food quality by 80 percent just by reminding all your staff not to talk badly about it.

No one would go into someone's home and insult the meal they're offered. And your staff can't be doing that in your communities either. Let me share two scenarios with you: A family tells the community relations manager that the food was bad. He agrees with them. Another family tells him the food was good, but he does not pass the information to the food service director. In fact, the two have never met.

How could staff learning better communication skills have helped in these examples? We need to get out of our own orbit and look at the bigger picture. You must lead your entire community to commit itself to a common purpose. We need to get all department leaders involved to support the food service team through the process. It is not just the foodservice department's burden to work through dining improvement. It needs to be shared by all staff.

Establishing clear, concise, confirmable, and challenging dining standards that support your community's vision, mission, and values serves as the foundation for consistent improvement. When standards are properly communicated and implemented, they create a framework that elevates every aspect of service delivery. The importance of these service standards extends far beyond simple operational procedures—they represent a commitment to dignity, safety, and quality of life for residents while supporting staff development and organizational success.

Service standards are the level of service we are committed to achieving under *every* circumstance. We know residents value high-quality service. Management's role is to make sure staff pull together and know what to do to deliver it. When there is no clear focus, everyone puts forth effort, but in the direction that seems right to them. What you end up with is something that looks and feels like misalignment and wasted energy. What's needed is to align all these energies through clear vision, mission, standards, goals, and expectations.

Many communities I talk with are using F-tags (a set of federal regulations used by the Centers for Medicare and Medicaid to survey and cite deficiencies in long-term care facilities), QAPI (Quality Assurance and Performance Improvement program) protocols, and government regulations as their standards. *But truly, these are the bare minimums.* If you want to remain competitive in this industry, you've got to do far better than the minimum.

As leaders, we need to be very clear about what great service looks like for current and future clientele. To do that, we must clearly define and set higher service standards. In the Kind Dining training, we start this process by writing what we call service statements. Service statements are the actions we will take to ensure the standards are both clear and incorporated. They describe what we intend to do to provide quality service. Service statements clarify our standards and define our vision so we can make it a reality.

Service statements clarify our standards and define our vision so we can make it a reality.

Resident Quality Of Life: The Heart Of Standardized Care

The primary beneficiaries of well-established standards are the residents themselves, whose quality of life depends on consistency and reliability in their daily experiences. Standardized care protocols ensure that residents receive consistent, high-quality service experiences that contribute significantly to their overall well-being. When dining services follow established standards, residents can anticipate predictable meal times, familiar food preparation methods, and consistent service delivery that creates a sense of comfort and security in their daily routines.

These standards also provide a framework for addressing individual preferences while maintaining operational efficiency. Rather than creating chaos through ad hoc accommodations, standardized processes can incorporate flexibility points where personalization occurs within established parameters. This approach honors the diverse backgrounds, cultural preferences, and individual tastes of residents while ensuring that nutritional needs and dietary requirements are consistently met across the community.

Standards should also be viewed as a roadmap to fulfilling the mission, vision, and values of the community. A unified mission and vision should articulate the direction you want your community to take. This is especially true with a customized dining mission statement. With the mission, you are sharing what is important and where the focus of the staff should be. If there is no clear line to the dining mission, vision, and values, leadership must step in to make this connection clear. Leveraging service standards in this capacity helps staff understand the alignment with that important target.

The dignity and respect that emerge from standardized service cannot be overstated. When staff members follow established protocols, residents experience a level of professionalism and attention to detail that reinforces their value as individuals. This consistency helps maintain residents' sense of autonomy and self-worth, crucial factors in successful aging and a community's sense of belonging.

Unfortunately, far too many healthcare executives neglect this step because it requires both time and effort. Time is a rare commodity for most leaders. However, there is a cost to not standardizing service. When you don't set standards for dining service, your staff do not have a clear target. Communicate clearly what is most important by using a standardized services tool.

When staff members follow established protocols, residents experience a level of professionalism and attention to detail that reinforces their value as individuals.

The Science Of Standardized Nutrition

Standardized nutritional protocols form the backbone of effective health management in senior care communities. These standards ensure that diverse dietary needs are systematically addressed, reducing the risk of malnutrition and weight-related health issues that can significantly affect resident health outcomes. When nutritional care follows established guidelines, it becomes easier to track patterns, identify concerns early, and implement interventions before minor issues become major health problems.

Standardized foodservice protocols ensure that the Flow of Food process—receiving, storing, preparing, cooking, and holding/serving, or sometimes cooling and reheating—meets the highest safety requirements, reducing the risk of foodborne illness. These standards also facilitate the management of medical dietary restrictions and specialized diets, ensuring that residents with conditions such as diabetes, heart disease, or swallowing difficulties receive appropriate nutritional support.

The ability to track resident nutritional intake becomes significantly more effective when standards are in place. Consistent documentation methods and measurement protocols allow care teams to monitor trends, identify declining appetite or nutritional status, and collaborate with healthcare providers to adjust care plans as needed. This systematic approach to nutritional monitoring can prevent serious health complications and support overall resident wellness.

Staff Development And Morale: Building Professional Excellence

Standardized service procedures and behaviors offer consistent training opportunities that help staff members develop professionally and build confidence in their abilities. When employees understand clearly what is expected and receive proper training to meet those expectations, they experience greater job satisfaction and professional pride. This sense of competence and confidence translates into better resident care and improved workplace morale.

Standards also create a sense of team unity and shared purpose. When all staff members follow the same protocols and pursue the same quality objectives, they develop a collaborative spirit that strengthens the entire team. This unity supports more effective performance management, as expectations are clear and consistent across the organization.

Resident Satisfaction And Retention

Predictable, reliable dining experiences contribute significantly to resident satisfaction and retention. When residents know they can count on consistent quality and service, they develop trust in the community and feel more secure in their living environment. Standardized approaches to addressing diverse dietary and cultural needs demonstrate respect for individual backgrounds while ensuring that all residents receive appropriate care.

This consistency in service delivery increases overall satisfaction with community living and reduces resident and family complaints. When problems do arise, standardized procedures provide clear protocols for resolution, ensuring that issues are addressed promptly and effectively. This reliability in both service delivery and problem resolution builds the trust essential to resident satisfaction and retention.

Integrating Standards With First Impressions

The first impression of a potential new resident, including that "wow" factor, is supported by service standards of behavior. How you appear sets the expectation for the experience before visitors even walk in the door. Your people are the face of the organization, and they shape the impression the community makes on anyone who first interacts with it.

The residents, both current and future, view the community through the way staff interact with them and each other. First impressions are not just experienced with a new visitor. There is a first impression at the start of a day or a meal. These are either opportunities to enforce good impressions of the community or highlight bad ones.

When staff understand what is expected of them, they have the ability to perform to meet those expectations. If they have not received training on those standards, they simply don't know and try the best they can. You can have staff try or train—there is a cost associated with both, but a better return on training versus trying.

The Daughter's Journey

Vicki Abbate has been the primary caretaker of her mother, who has dementia, for several years. The family decided to move her mom closer to Vicki, as she was retired and could interact with a memory care community and visit her mom more often.

She looked at twelve different locations, and many of the first impressions were lacking. For instance, there was no one to greet her at several locations when she arrived. Some of the community's tour guides didn't know her name, let alone her mother's. And many did not interact with the current residents during the tour.

The list was narrowed down to two communities, and Vicki put her mom's name on both waiting lists. When the first location had room for her mom in memory care, she noticed a few things. There were no fewer than five new administrators/executive directors in the two years her mom lived here. Required protocols, like having quarterly care plan meetings about her mother's care, had to be fought for.

She also noticed the staff were never invited to be part of the care team. As she stated, "It is about me and my mom. And I am looking for a partner in her care—someone who will treat me well at this moment as a family member and who could treat me well later on if I became a resident."

The final straw to move her mom came when she had an accident and ended up in the hospital.

"I was out of town, but we had family members who could come to the hospital if she was admitted. The staff member never called to tell me which hospital my mom was being admitted to, and my mom stayed overnight at the hospital by herself. That must have been so stressful for her—not just because she has dementia but because she is vulnerable. When I asked the staff member later why she didn't call, her response was that her shift ended."

The community her mom is currently living in is providing care, civility, and courtesies that are above and beyond. She said, "They always offer me a meal or beverage whenever I visit, and they never know when I or one of my sisters is going to show up. I have learned it's best to keep it random, sometimes on weekends, sometimes during dinner, or in the morning on my way to the store.

"All the caregivers know my mom and know me. Even the concierge knows all the residents and how they are doing on any particular day. I feel like I am part of their team, and giving great care to my mom is the end goal. The most interesting part is that this community is less expensive while being brand new."

The standards of service are different, and this can be seen in how residents and their families are viewed, greeted, and treated. The staff have standards from the moment someone walks in the door, and it shows in how they approach their work and one another.

Setting clear, concise, challenging, and confirming service standards in senior care communities represents far more than operational efficiency; it embodies a commitment to excellence that touches every aspect of resident life. These service standards create the foundation for quality care, staff development, and organizational success.

When properly implemented, they transform communities from mere providers into communities of belonging where residents can thrive, staff can develop professionally, and organizations can achieve their mission of providing exceptional care. The investment in developing and maintaining these service standards pays dividends in resident satisfaction, staff morale, operational efficiency, and long-term organizational success.

13

Hiring For Hospitality Across Departments

Every position you hire for has importance. If it weren't critical to your operation, you would not be spending money on it! Investing in operations can only get you so far. Hiring well sets you up for true dining and community transformation.

The quality of service in senior living and post-acute care communities fundamentally depends on the people who provide it. While technical skills and certifications are important, the most successful senior care organizations recognize that exceptional care emerges from hiring individuals who possess not only competence but also genuine compassion, emotional intelligence, and a deep commitment to service. Establishing clear, challenging, and confirming hiring standards ensures that every new team member contributes to a unique culture of accountability that enhances resident quality of life, supports organizational mission, and creates sustainable success.

The transformation of senior care begins with recognizing that hiring decisions represent strategic investments in care quality rather than simple staffing solutions. When communities approach hiring with comprehensive standards that prioritize character alongside credentials, they build teams capable of delivering the personalized, dignified care that residents deserve. These standards create a framework for identifying candidates who are willing to learn and view caregiving as a calling rather than just employment, ultimately resulting in higher resident satisfaction, improved health outcomes, and stronger performance.

Just Come And Visit Me

A story I was told was about a senior living community in Maine. The daughter wanted to move her father to the community where she had just been hired (a competitor of where he currently lived) so that she could see him every day.

Within a week, he had moved back to the original community. He shared this observation, "Nursing care is nursing care wherever you are. Hospitality is the differentiator. The absence of hospitality is startling once you have experienced it. I told my daughter she could just come and visit me after her shift."

He saw the marked difference in civility with who was providing the service. In fact, he had a private room at the other community and came back to a shared room because of how he felt about the people who worked there. The people, and how they cared, made the impact to come back.

Cultural Alignment That Supports A Quality Dining Culture

The most critical aspect of hiring in senior care communities involves identifying people whose personal values and professional motivations align with the commitment to exceptional care. This alignment begins with seeking individuals who demonstrate empathy in their interactions with others. Empathetic caregivers (who also serve meals) naturally prioritize resident dignity, comfort, and well-being, creating the foundation for meaningful relationships that enhance quality of life.

A service-oriented mindset represents another essential characteristic that hiring standards must prioritize. Candidates who naturally focus on meeting others' needs and finding satisfaction in service delivery will thrive in senior care environments where resident needs must always take precedence. This orientation goes beyond simple job performance to encompass a fundamental approach to work that views service as personally fulfilling and professionally meaningful.

Communities undergoing a dining transformation or refining their approach must carefully assess candidates' alignment with evolving core values. This assessment ensures that new hires will support rather than undermine culture change initiatives. When hiring standards include specific evaluation of value alignment, you can build teams that collectively embody the mission and vision for exceptional care.

The prioritization of emotional intelligence over purely technical skills represents a strategic recognition that senior care is fundamentally about human relationships. While technical competence can be taught, emotional intelligence—the ability to understand, manage, and respond appropriately to emotions—is more difficult to develop. Candidates with high emotional intelligence can navigate the complex emotional landscape of senior care, supporting residents through challenges while maintaining their own emotional well-being.

Perhaps most importantly, hiring standards must identify candidates who view caregiving as a calling rather than simply employment. These individuals bring intrinsic motivation that sustains them through challenges and drives them to continuously improve their care delivery.

Their commitment extends beyond job requirements to encompass a personal investment in resident welfare and community success.

I have seen that when we recruit for hospitality, a crisis can be handled with grace and agility. In my own state of Oregon, I saw senior care communities work together to evacuate when wildfires raged and work to get the residents back into their community and familiar routines. When there is disruption, having staff who understand the service aspect of their work can make all the difference.

Technical And Soft Skills: A Balance Of Competence And Character

Communication abilities represent perhaps the most critical skill set for senior care professionals. Effective caregivers must communicate clearly with residents who may have hearing difficulties, cognitive challenges, or emotional needs. They must also collaborate effectively with family members, healthcare providers, and team members. Hiring standards should include specific assessment of verbal and nonverbal communication skills, active listening abilities, and the capacity to adapt communication styles to different audiences and situations.

Problem-solving skills are essential in senior care environments where unexpected situations arise regularly. Candidates must demonstrate the ability to think critically, assess situations quickly, and develop appropriate solutions that prioritize resident safety and well-being. Evaluation of problem-solving abilities should include both technical problem-solving and the more nuanced challenges of addressing resident concerns, family dynamics, and team conflicts.

The ability to work effectively in team environments is crucial for senior care success. Care delivery requires seamless coordination among multiple staff members, including maintenance crews, care managers, nursing teams, dietary staff, housekeeping, and recreation and wellness coordinators. Candidates must demonstrate not only the ability to collaborate but also the flexibility to adapt their working style to complement team dynamics and support collective goals.

Capacity for continuous learning has become increasingly important as senior care evolves to incorporate new technologies, care approaches, and regulatory requirements. Hiring standards should assess candidates' openness to learning, their track record of professional development, and their ability to adapt to changing circumstances. This evaluation helps ensure that new hires will grow with the community rather than becoming obstacles to progress.

The willingness to receive and implement feedback is crucial in senior care settings where continuous improvement is essential for resident safety and satisfaction. Candidates who demonstrate coachability and responsiveness to feedback will be able to refine their care delivery based on resident needs, family input, and supervisory guidance. This characteristic is especially valuable for candidates who may be new to senior care but possess the fundamental attributes needed for success.

Setting The Foundation For Success

I will get into training in a later chapter, but the importance cannot be overstated. Comprehensive training programs represent a critical investment in care quality and staff success. These programs should address not only technical skills and regulatory requirements but also the community's specific care philosophy, communication standards, and cultural expectations. When training is comprehensive and well-designed, it ensures that all team members share a common understanding of care standards and organizational values.

Clear performance expectations eliminate confusion and provide new hires with specific goals and standards to achieve. These expectations should encompass both technical competencies and interpersonal skills, creating a comprehensive framework for success. When expectations are clearly communicated and consistently applied, they support both individual development and overall quality standards.

Performance expectations are also tied to the job description and duties. One way to ensure the job description accurately reflects the work is to have the staff member create a list of their duties and assigned tasks. I have seen management think a task was in alignment with staff member A when, in fact, it was already handled (and well) by staff member B. This could be done when a new staff member joins the team or scheduled at different times during the year.

Ongoing skills development ensures that team members continue to grow professionally and remain current with best practices in senior care. This commitment to continuous learning demonstrates the investment in staff development while ensuring that care delivery continues to improve over time. Technology can facilitate consistent training delivery, ensuring that all team members receive the same high-quality instruction regardless of scheduling constraints or geographical limitations.

Communities can create supportive learning environments where mistakes are viewed as learning opportunities rather than failures. This encourages risk-taking and innovation in care delivery, fosters creativity and continuous improvement, and maintains the high standards necessary for resident safety and satisfaction.

A Strategic Approach To Team Building

The principle of prioritizing character over credentials represents a fundamental shift in how many communities approach hiring. While credentials provide essential information about candidates' training and experience, character determines how they will use those credentials in the service of resident care. Communities that prioritize character often find that they can develop technical skills more easily than they can instill compassion, integrity, and commitment.

Looking beyond resumes to assess individual potential requires hiring managers to evaluate candidates' capacity for growth, intrinsic motivation, and alignment with community values. This approach recognizes that the best candidates may not always have the most impressive credentials but possess the fundamental characteristics needed for success in senior care environments.

By creating holistic assessment processes, communities ensure that hiring decisions look at all relevant factors rather than focusing narrowly on specific qualifications. These processes should evaluate technical skills, interpersonal abilities, cultural fit, growth potential, and commitment to service. Holistic assessment provides a more complete picture of candidates' potential contributions.

Building talent pipelines rather than simply filling immediate needs represents a strategic approach to staffing that anticipates future needs and opportunities. This approach involves developing relationships with potential candidates, creating career development pathways, and maintaining connections with strong candidates who may not be immediately available. Talent pipelines ensure that communities have access to quality candidates when positions become available.

It is vital to view hiring as a strategic investment in care quality, as it recognizes that staffing decisions have long-term implications for success. This perspective encourages communities to invest time and resources in comprehensive hiring processes that identify the best possible candidates rather than simply filling positions quickly. When hiring is viewed as an investment rather than an expense, you are more likely to achieve your care quality goals.

An Administrator Becomes A Coach

Sarah was the first administrator who became a Kind Dining instructor, and I am still in contact with her over twenty-five years later. She sent me a card, and it read, "The years doing Kind Dining with you are probably the best years of my career." I wish I could take credit, but she was and is an inspirational leader with a servant's heart. Whoever hired her did a fantastic service for their entire organization.

Leaders like Sarah are passionate and committed to accomplishing great things; they see unlimited potential. They value and invest in the education, personal growth, and individual success of the people they have around them and invite them to work hard together. Her employees were fired up to help her achieve the culture change goals they laid out, and to transform their dining environments to better serve their residents and families. They far exceeded their goals for many years running. In essence, they hired well.

Strategic hiring standards for senior care communities go far beyond personnel policies—they embody a commitment to excellence that touches every aspect of organizational performance. Success in senior care hiring requires viewing each staffing decision as an investment in care quality, organizational culture, and long-term sustainability. When these principles guide hiring practices, organizations create environments where exceptional care becomes not just a goal but a natural outcome of having the right people in the right roles with the proper support.

14

Continual Hospitality Training For All

The landscape of senior care has been fundamentally transformed by recent global events, particularly the pandemic, which exposed critical vulnerabilities in how residential communities serve their most susceptible residents. Research indicates that during the early months of the pandemic, 56 percent of older adults experienced significant isolation,[30] with residential home residents facing even more severe challenges. Even post-pandemic data show that one-third of older adults sometimes or often feel isolated from others.

The prevalence of severe loneliness among older people living in long-term care homes is at least double that of community-dwelling populations,[31] ranging from 22 percent to 42 percent, compared with 10 percent for community residents. These statistics underscore a fundamental truth: The quality of care delivered in senior communities directly correlates with the training, competence, and engagement of the staff who provide it.

Against this backdrop of increased vulnerability and heightened care needs, the importance of continual staff training has never been more critical. Hospitality training represents far more than a regulatory requirement or operational necessity—it serves as the cornerstone of quality care delivery, resident mental health, and organizational sustainability. There are clear multifaceted benefits of comprehensive, ongoing training programs, and they constitute one of the most valuable investments senior care communities can make.

Direct Performance Improvements

The most immediate and visible impact of continual training manifests in direct performance improvements across all aspects of care delivery. Well-trained staff make fewer errors, respond more effectively to emergencies, and provide higher-quality care experiences for residents. When all staff members receive regular, comprehensive training, they develop the competencies necessary to recognize subtle changes in resident conditions, respond appropriately to behavioral challenges, and implement evidence-based care protocols effectively.

Moreover, continual training ensures more consistent resident and family member experiences across all shifts and departments. When all staff members receive standardized hospitality training on communication techniques, care protocols, and resident rights, they can deliver uniform service quality regardless of individual differences in background or experience. This consistency becomes particularly crucial given the high turnover rates in senior care communities,[32] where maintaining service standards despite frequent staff changes presents ongoing challenges.

The confidence and competence that emerge from comprehensive training programs create a positive feedback loop that benefits both staff and residents.

As Will Guidara points out in his national best-selling book, *Unreasonable Hospitality*, "When you create a hospitality-first culture, everything about your business improves because hospitality is a selfish pleasure. It feels great to make other people feel good."[33]

Confident staff members are more likely to engage proactively with residents, identify potential issues early, and collaborate effectively with healthcare professionals. This increased competence translates directly into improved resident satisfaction scores and better health outcomes.

The Business Case For Training Investment

The financial benefits of continual hospitality training extend far beyond the immediate costs of program implementation, creating substantial returns on investment that impact every aspect of operations. The most significant financial benefit comes from reduced staff turnover costs, which are among the most significant expenses facing senior care communities. Data indicate that the annual turnover rate among senior living and post-acute care workers is as high as 85 percent across all positions,[34] with the average cost of replacing a single nursing assistant estimated between $3,000 to as much as $7,000 when considering recruitment, training, and productivity losses.

Research demonstrates that facilities investing in comprehensive training programs can achieve a 10 to 20 percent reduction in staff turnover.[35] For a hundred-bed facility with eighty direct care staff members, this reduction could save between $240,000 and $560,000 in turnover-related costs alone. These savings result from reduced recruitment expenses, decreased training replacement costs, and improved productivity as experienced staff members remain with the community longer.

The impact of training on reducing potential liability risks cannot be overstated. Facilities with well-trained staff experience fewer incidents of medical errors, falls, and other preventable adverse events that can result in costly litigation and regulatory sanctions. Insurance premiums often reflect claims history, meaning that communities with strong training programs and better safety records may qualify for reduced insurance costs over time.

Enhanced operational efficiency represents another significant financial benefit of continual training. Staff members who understand proper food procedures, utilize equipment effectively, and communicate efficiently reduce waste, minimize resource consumption, and optimize workflow processes. This efficiency translates into cost savings across multiple operational areas, from reduced food waste to improved staff productivity.

Training investments also enhance community reputation, directly impacting occupancy rates and revenue generation. In my first book, *Hospitality for Boomers*,[36] I share that when there is a higher satisfaction with the dining experience, you win over residents and family members. They, in turn, are more likely to recommend your community to others. Communities known for high-quality care and well-trained staff attract more prospective residents and their families, helping maintain high occupancy levels. In competitive markets, a reputation for excellence can command premium pricing and reduce marketing costs as word-of-mouth referrals increase.

Building A Committed Workforce

The relationship between training and staff engagement extends far beyond skill development to encompass fundamental aspects of job satisfaction, professional growth, and staff commitment. When communities invest in continual training, they demonstrate a tangible commitment to employee development that resonates deeply with staff members at all levels. According to Cara Siletto,[37] this is a mindset shift that is critical in today's workforce.

Training programs that focus on skill development and career advancement foster a sense of professional purpose, helping combat the burnout commonly experienced in senior care settings. Staff members who feel they are growing professionally and developing new competencies are more likely to remain engaged with their work and committed to their community. This engagement translates into better resident care, improved workplace morale, and stronger team cohesion.

The professional development opportunities provided through comprehensive training programs help staff members envision long-term career paths. Rather than viewing their positions as temporary employment, staff members begin to see opportunities for advancement, specialization, and professional growth. This perspective shift significantly impacts retention rates and creates a more stable, experienced workforce.

Training that addresses the emotional and psychological aspects of caregiving helps staff members develop resilience and coping strategies essential for long-term success in senior care. Programs that teach stress management, communication skills, and self-care techniques reduce burnout and help staff members maintain their passion for caregiving throughout their careers.

The social connections formed during training programs also contribute to staff retention. When staff members participate in learning experiences together, they develop stronger professional relationships and a greater sense of belonging. These connections create informal support networks that help staff members navigate challenges and maintain job satisfaction.

Strive For Long-Term Success

The strategic value of continual training extends beyond immediate operational improvements to encompass long-term development and competitive positioning. Comprehensive training programs create a talent development pipeline that enables communities to promote from within, reducing recruitment costs and ensuring continuity of the culture and values.

Training initiatives that encourage innovation and continuous learning foster adaptability, which becomes increasingly valuable in a rapidly changing healthcare environment. Staff members who are accustomed to learning new procedures, adapting to new technologies, and embracing best practices are better positioned to help their communities respond to regulatory changes, market pressures, and evolving resident needs.

The development of internal leadership potential through training programs creates succession planning opportunities that strengthen sustainability. When staff members receive leadership development training, they recognize their own individual value and will apply for supervisory and management positions, ensuring leadership continuity.

Communities with strong training programs enhance their reputation within the industry, making them more attractive to high-quality job candidates. This reputation advantage creates competitive staffing advantages that become particularly valuable in tight labor markets. Companies that invest in their staff attract candidates committed to professional growth and excellence in care delivery.

The support for long-term strategic goals through training initiatives ensures that staff development aligns with current objectives. Whether the goal is expanding services, implementing new technologies, or achieving accreditation standards, well-trained staff members are essential to successful strategy execution.

Focus On The Strategies Behind Training

The most successful senior living and post-acute care communities approach hospitality training as a strategic investment rather than a necessary expense. This philosophy requires viewing training as an integral component of the culture rather than an add-on activity. Communities that embrace this perspective create learning-centered cultures where continuous improvement becomes the norm rather than the exception.

Supporting both individual and community growth through training initiatives requires programs that address personal development needs while advancing current objectives. This dual focus ensures that training investments benefit both staff members and the community, creating sustainable value that extends beyond immediate skill development.

Recognizing training as a continuous process rather than a one-time event enables the adaptation of programs to changing needs, emerging best practices, and evolving regulatory requirements. This continuous approach ensures that staff competencies remain current and relevant throughout their careers.

This philosophy requires viewing training as an integral component of the culture rather than an add-on activity.

The Impact Of The Investment

The evidence overwhelmingly demonstrates that continual training represents one of the most valuable investments senior care communities can make. The direct performance improvements, financial returns, enhanced staff engagement, and strategic benefits create a compelling case for comprehensive training programs that extend far beyond basic compliance requirements.

In an industry facing unprecedented challenges with staffing shortages, regulatory pressures, and increasing resident acuity, communities that prioritize continual training position themselves for long-term success.

And communities with well-trained, engaged staff provide better care, achieve better outcomes, and maintain stronger financial performance than those that treat training as an afterthought.

The pandemic's impact on loneliness and isolation in senior living communities has only intensified the importance of having skilled, compassionate staff who can provide not just medical care but emotional support and human connection. Training programs that develop these competencies become essential investments in resident well-being and overall community sustainability.

Starting in the dining room is key, as it is the most vital and visible area to make a first impression. We can continually improve our results as staff keep learning and practicing this work in alignment with the organization's business goals.

As the aging services industry continues to evolve, embracing comprehensive training as a strategic priority will create a competitive advantage that extends across all aspects of operations. The question is not whether you can afford to invest in continual training, but whether you can afford not to make this critical investment in your most valuable resource: your people.

When Hiring Well Isn't Readily Available

Sarah McEvoy has been in long-term care her entire career, from dietary aide to executive and everything in between. For the last thirty-six years of her career, she worked as a nursing home administrator. And she will tell you that if you want to aspire to a new level of service and success in your community, you need the skills to go with it.

She shared many times, "The environment prevents you from being able to do all things well. In the world now, there aren't enough staff members. So, you can't always hire well, but you can always train well.

You can always say that, while the best candidates aren't out there right now, I do have these candidates. And I am confident that if I do this hospitality training well, I can bring them up to the level that I need them to be."

She also shared that innovation comes from people empowered to think outside current parameters and get creative, which doesn't come with a large price tag or a need for resources.

One story she shares is that of the soggy toast problem. "We had an issue with the post-acute care residents, when the food trays were passed, that the toast would be cold and a bit soggy. One of the members of the team came up with the idea of having a toaster and bread on each floor."

When the trays came up, either a dietary aide or a housekeeping member trained in food safety would start the toast for residents who requested it. They would then bring the toast into the rooms, warm and crisp. That small shift not only made the residents happy but also took very little time and effort from the staff and freed up the kitchen from having to make a ton of toast that ended up getting tossed.

Innovation and inspiration can easily come from within when staff are invited to work on the problem and become part of the solution.

15

Coaching To Reinforce Behaviors

The art of coaching in communities that residents call their home represents a delicate balance between professional development and compassionate guidance. It requires leaders to navigate complex interpersonal dynamics while maintaining the highest standards of care delivery. Unlike traditional corporate environments where coaching might focus primarily on productivity metrics, senior living coaching must encompass the emotional, psychological, and technical aspects of caregiving that directly impact vulnerable residents' well-being.

Building The Framework For Success

The cornerstone of effective coaching lies in creating supportive, nonpunitive feedback environments where staff members feel safe to acknowledge challenges, explore solutions, and grow professionally. This approach requires a fundamental shift from traditional disciplinary models toward developmental frameworks that view mistakes as learning opportunities rather than failures requiring punishment. When staff members operate in environments free from fear of being judged, they become more willing to seek guidance, admit uncertainties, and engage in honest self-reflection about their performance.

The focus on positive reinforcement forms the bedrock of successful coaching relationships. Positive feedback is significantly more effective than criticism in driving behavioral change and performance improvement. In senior care settings, where staff members often face emotionally challenging situations and high-stress environments, positive reinforcement becomes particularly crucial for maintaining morale and motivation. This approach doesn't ignore areas needing improvement but frames development opportunities within contexts of growth and potential rather than deficiency and failure.

Developing individualized coaching approaches requires leaders to recognize that each staff member brings unique backgrounds, experiences, and learning styles to their roles. A certified nursing assistant with twenty years of experience requires different coaching strategies than a recent graduate entering the field for the first time. Similarly, staff members from different cultural backgrounds may respond differently to various coaching techniques, requiring adaptation of approaches while maintaining consistent standards and expectations.

The recognition of unique learning styles becomes particularly important in senior care environments where staff may have diverse educational backgrounds and varying levels of formal training. Some individuals learn best through hands-on demonstration, while others prefer written instructions or verbal explanations. Effective leaders assess these preferences and adjust their teaching methods accordingly, ensuring that all staff members can access and internalize the information necessary for success.

Building trust through consistent, compassionate guidance creates the foundation for all other coaching activities. Trust develops through reliable, predictable interactions where leaders demonstrate genuine concern for staff members' professional and personal well-being. This trust enables honest conversations about performance challenges, creates openness to feedback, and fosters the vulnerability necessary for meaningful growth and development.

The alignment of coaching with the mission, vision, and values ensures that individual development supports broader goals while maintaining authenticity in leadership interactions. When coaching reflects the community's commitment to dignity, respect, and excellence, staff understand that their professional development contributes to meaningful purposes beyond personal advancement. This alignment creates coherence between individual growth and the mission of the community, strengthening commitment to both personal excellence and institutional values.

Excellence Through Recognition

The identification and celebration of specific positive behaviors create powerful reinforcement cycles that encourage continued excellence while providing clear examples of desired performance. Rather than offering generic praise, effective coaches identify specific actions, decisions, or approaches that exemplify quality care and professional excellence. This specificity helps staff members understand exactly what behaviors contribute to success and provides concrete examples they can replicate in future situations.

Even with agency staff, you can hold them to many of the same standards. An example would be tracking all staff and ensuring they arrive so that they are on the floor when their shift starts. Agency staff can be held to that same standard. This creates a team camaraderie and inclusivity.

Providing immediate, constructive feedback ensures that coaching moments occur when they have maximum impact on learning and behavior modification. The temporal proximity between action and feedback strengthens the connection between behavior and outcome, making the coaching more effective and memorable. In senior care environments where situations change rapidly, immediate feedback also prevents the reinforcement of incorrect behaviors or the missed opportunity to acknowledge excellent performance.

The use of specific, observable examples in coaching conversations eliminates ambiguity and creates clear understanding of expectations and achievements. Rather than discussing abstract concepts like "better communication," effective leaders reference specific instances where staff members demonstrated excellent communication skills, explaining precisely what made those interactions effective. This specificity helps staff understand not just what to do, but how to do it consistently.

Clear performance expectations provide the framework within which coaching conversations occur. When staff members understand exactly what constitutes excellent performance, they can better assess their own progress and identify areas for improvement. These expectations must be specific, measurable, and achievable while maintaining the high standards necessary for quality care delivery.

Peer recognition programs can harness the power of social reinforcement to encourage positive behaviors throughout the organization. When staff recognize and celebrate each other's achievements, it creates a culture of mutual support and shared excellence. Peer recognition often carries special significance because it comes from individuals who understand the challenges and complexities of the work firsthand.

Designing meaningful reward systems requires understanding what motivates individual staff members and creating recognition that feels authentic and valuable. While financial rewards may not always be feasible, meaningful recognition might include preferred scheduling, professional development opportunities, or public acknowledgment of achievements. The key is ensuring that rewards align with individual motivations and the mission, vision, and values of the community.

Honoring Unique Potential

The recognition of individual learning capabilities requires leadership to assess each staff member's unique strengths, challenges, and potential for growth. This assessment involves understanding not just what individuals can do currently, but what they might be capable of achieving with appropriate support and development. Recognizing individual capabilities helps coaches tailor their approaches and set realistic yet challenging goals.

If a community wishes to address specific skill gaps, it requires leaders to identify precise areas where improvement is needed and develop targeted strategies for building those competencies. This approach moves beyond general performance concerns to focus on specific, observable skills that can be developed through practice, training, and feedback. Addressing skill gaps systematically ensures that development efforts are efficient and effective.

Individual motivation drives each staff member and it is critical to understand what makes each staff member go the extra mile. Some individuals are motivated by recognition, others by autonomy, and still others by opportunities for advancement or learning. Effective leaders identify these triggers and use them to enhance the coaching relationship and drive performance improvement.

Personal learning preferences means that individuals process information and develop skills in different ways. Some people learn best through visual demonstration, others through hands-on practice, and still others through verbal instruction or written materials. Respecting these preferences and incorporating them into coaching strategies enhances learning effectiveness and demonstrates respect for individual differences.

Leaders can build individual confidence by helping staff members recognize their own capabilities and potential for growth. This includes acknowledging achievements, providing appropriate challenges, and supporting staff members through difficulties. Confident staff members are more likely to take initiative, seek feedback, and engage in continuous learning.

Environments For Growth

The creation of positive coaching environments requires deliberate attention to both physical and psychological factors that influence staff members' comfort and openness. Physical factors might include private spaces for conversations, comfortable seating arrangements, and elimination of barriers that create hierarchical feelings. Psychological factors include tone of voice, body language, and the overall approach to coaching conversations.

The support of emotional resilience helps staff members develop the psychological resources necessary to handle the challenges inherent in senior care work. This support might include stress management techniques, emotional regulation strategies, and resources for dealing with difficult situations. Emotionally resilient staff members are better equipped to learn from feedback, adapt to changes, and maintain high performance under pressure.

By building trust through consistent support, leaders demonstrate reliability, authenticity, and genuine concern for staff members' well-being. Trust develops through repeated positive interactions where senior leaders show they are committed to staff members' success and development. This trust creates the foundation for honest feedback, vulnerable conversations, and meaningful growth.

How Good Can Your Company Get?

The alignment of coaching with core values ensures that individual development supports both the culture and mission. This alignment requires leaders to understand and embody community values while helping staff members see how their personal growth contributes to company goals. When coaching reflects those values, it reinforces culture and creates consistency across all staff levels.

Demonstrating commitment to staff growth through coaching sends powerful messages about values and priorities. When community leaders invest time, resources, and attention into staff development, they communicate that people are valued and that continual improvement is expected and supported. This focus creates commitment, motivation, and pride in being a partner working within that community.

If a community wants to transform its culture, they must collectively have development conversations and support. These shifts must become integral to how the community operates rather than additional activities. This integration involves incorporating coaching into regular supervision, performance management, and strategic planning processes. When coaching becomes part of the DNA, it influences all interactions and decisions.

Supporting a continuous improvement culture through coaching creates environments where learning, growth, and excellence become ongoing characteristics. Continuous improvement cultures encourage experimentation, learning from mistakes, and constant striving for better outcomes. Coaching supports this culture by providing the feedback, support, and encouragement necessary for sustained improvement.

Kathryn Kindopp can view the cows at the bottom of the hill from her office as a nursing home administrator where she has worked for thirty years. She was recruited from Canada to improve customer service from all angles. But who you consider your customer can be more than you think.

She shared, "During our training, I ask the staff, who are our customers? And of course, everyone's going to say, 'your residents.' And I'd say, "and who else?' 'Families.' 'Who else?' 'Visitors.' Inevitably, everyone forgets that we, as staff, are customers of one another."

If you look at the organization and the members as part of the customer experience, there is an inherent sense of belonging and purpose. Good leaders will always want to improve the external customer experience. But what about the internal one? How we treat each other is seen by our residents and visitors. If we treat each other with kindness and respect, we will move that civility outward to anyone who interacts with us, and people will see that.

Kathryn shared another story about always having a smile. "We have a saying: Our smile is everything. You would not think that would make an impact. One day, the EMT bringing one of our residents back commented that they like interacting with our staff because we always have a smile. If you think no one notices, you would be mistaken."

The Cost Of Incivility

There is a cost for allowing incivility in the workplace. In research published by Christine Porath and Christine Pearson in *Harvard Business Review*,[38] there is an impact on individuals in the workplace and their personal productivity.

In their findings, there is a reduction in work effort and quality and even higher turnover when incivility is left unchecked. In many ways, this is enforcing bad behaviors that degrade community and connection. There is also a negative impact on customer service within the community, with nearly a quarter of people surveyed admitting to taking their personal frustrations out on customers.

Understanding the importance of these seemingly innocent lapses of kindness, courtesy, and civility is crucial to maintaining healthy relationships. Porath and Pearson's research indicates that the increased stress of a confrontational workplace (and I have seen the worst displays of uncivil behaviors between nursing departments and food service departments) increases doctor visits, sick days, and staff turnover.

They also argue other, even more subtle behaviors aren't tracked as consequences to uncivil behaviors:

- 48 percent of employees surveyed who experienced uncivil behaviors said they intentionally decreased their work effort
- 38 percent decreased the quality of their work
- 78 percent of employees said their commitment to the organization itself declined
- 63 percent lost work time avoiding the other person/offender
- And 25 percent admitted to actually taking their frustration out on customers

In every instance, you are reinforcing some type of behavior, whether you do it purposely or not. What is this incivility costing you and what are you paying when you miss training opportunities?

The Transformative Power Of Compassionate Coaching

By implementing robust, compassionate coaching approaches, senior living and post-acute care communities can achieve transformative outcomes that extend far beyond individual performance improvement. These approaches elevate service standards by developing staff members who are skilled, confident, and committed to excellence. They support staff professional development by creating pathways for growth and advancement that align with both individual aspirations and community needs.

The meaningful performance improvements that result from effective coaching create ripple effects, influencing resident satisfaction, family confidence, and regulatory compliance. These improvements are sustainable because they are rooted in genuine development rather than external pressure or temporary interventions.

The ultimate goal is transforming coaching from a traditional performance management tool to a powerful, supportive mechanism for individual and community growth that directly enhances resident care quality.

When you invest in developing your people, you create cultures of belonging that attract quality staff, retain valuable employees, and deliver exceptional care to the residents you serve. This investment in human potential represents one of the most valuable strategies for achieving sustainable excellence in senior living communities.

The Door Took My Mom Out

I heard a story from my good friend about an incident at a senior living community. A staff worker was exiting the breakroom and did not open the door slowly. There was a resident—my friend's mom—just on the other side of the door, walking to her room. The door took her mom out.

She ended up in the hospital and made a full recovery. The community got cited and they were required to add a window into the door so the staff could see if someone was passing by the door. However, both the staff member and leadership blamed the resident. Months went by and the window was not added to the door (my friend paid attention to that).

My friend understood that it was an accident but instead of taking responsibility, the leadership enforced the wrong behavior. My friend did not wait to see if another resident would get taken out by the same door. She moved her mother as soon as possible from that community.

This may have nothing to do with dining, but the lesson is still the same: What behaviors are you reinforcing with your staff? And what future behaviors will develop as a result?

This investment in human potential represents one of the most valuable strategies for achieving sustainable excellence in senior living communities.

16

The Next Chapter

The name of my book is intentional. Senior living and post-acute care communities today can't dispense food like medicine.

I was at a rehab center doing my focus group meetings with residents for my original research. I asked the residents how their experiences were with the meal service.

One resident looked at me and she said, "Have you ever been to a restaurant, and the waitress just kind of threw the plate down at you? That is happening here. We don't want that to happen. We want to be treated as real people."

Without training, there are many times when staff who aren't serving meals as their primary job get so focused on their schedule or personal agenda that they unconsciously throw the meal down instead of presenting it.

With training, you know you have time to take five more seconds to politely say, "Mrs. Smith, here's your roasted chicken, green beans, and mashed potatoes. Is there anything else I may get for you?" Because

Mrs. Smith is living in her home, and is an honored member of this community. Serving her is not an annoyance that you have to get through.

From Care Recipients To Empowered Partners

The landscape of senior living and post-acute care continues to undergo a fundamental transformation that challenges decades of traditional care models. As we stand at the intersection of technological advancement, evolving generational expectations, and a deeper understanding of human wellness, senior living and post-acute care communities are reimagining their role from institutional care providers to collaborative partners in residents' journeys toward fulfillment and independence. This shift represents more than operational changes—it embodies a philosophical revolution that places resident agency, personal choice, and meaningful engagement at the heart of the senior living experience.

The Digital Revolution In Senior Care

The integration of sophisticated technology into senior living and post-acute care environments is creating unprecedented opportunities for personalization that were unimaginable just a decade ago. At the forefront of this transformation is the implementation of predictive analytics in dining services, where artificial intelligence systems analyze individual preferences, dietary restrictions, nutritional needs, and even mood patterns to curate customized meal experiences. These systems learn from residents' choices over time, adapting to seasonal preferences, health changes, and evolving tastes to create dining experiences that feel both luxurious and deeply personal.

Digital platforms are emerging as powerful tools that return control to residents' hands, allowing them to manage their schedules, communicate with family, access community resources, and make choices about their daily experiences through intuitive interfaces. These platforms represent a departure from the one-size-fits-all approach that has historically characterized senior living, instead offering residents the ability to customize their environment, services, and interactions according to their individual preferences and comfort levels.

The technology revolution in senior living and post-acute care extends beyond mere convenience—it addresses the fundamental human need for autonomy and self-determination. When residents can control their environment through smart home technologies, access information independently, and communicate their preferences through digital channels, they maintain a sense of autonomy that traditional care models often inadvertently diminish. But remember, with any technology, there is a real human behind it. Technology doesn't replace the human connection—it enhances it.

Holistic Wellness And Integrative Care Models

The evolution from medical-model care to comprehensive wellness approaches represents perhaps the most significant philosophical shift in senior living and post-acute care. This transformation acknowledges that optimal aging encompasses far more than the absence of disease—it requires attention to physical vitality, mental acuity, emotional well-being, social connection, and spiritual fulfillment. Progressive communities are implementing integrative care models that view nutrition not merely as sustenance but as a powerful tool for both preventative health and therapeutic intervention.

This holistic approach recognizes that meaningful engagement, continuous learning, and purposeful activities are not luxury amenities but essential components of healthy aging. Communities are developing programming that connects residents with opportunities for lifelong learning, creative expression, and community contribution.

Whether through intergenerational programs that allow residents to mentor younger people, continuing education opportunities that stimulate intellectual curiosity, or volunteer initiatives that provide outlets for giving back, these programs acknowledge that purpose and engagement are fundamental to human flourishing at any age.

The integration of wellness philosophy into daily operations means that every aspect of community life, from architectural design to meal planning, from activity programming to staff interactions, is evaluated through the lens of holistic well-being. This approach creates environments where residents feel valued not just as care recipients but as whole individuals with diverse interests, capabilities, and contributions to make.

Generational Expectations And Transformation

The arrival of baby boomers and Generation X in senior living and post-acute care communities brings with it a seismic shift in expectations that will reshape the industry for decades to come. These generations, having experienced unprecedented prosperity, technological advancement, and consumer empowerment throughout their lives, approach senior living with expectations that mirror their lifelong experiences in hospitality and service industries.

The demand for resort-style living experiences reflects more than a desire for luxury—it represents an expectation of choice, quality, and respect that these generations have come to expect. This includes flexible living arrangements that can adapt to changing needs without requiring disruptive relocations, customizable services that respect individual preferences, and transparent communication that treats residents as informed consumers rather than passive recipients of care.

The emphasis on maintaining independence while accessing support represents a delicate balance that successful communities must master.

These residents want the security and convenience of professional services while retaining the autonomy to make decisions about their daily lives, social interactions, and personal care. This requires communities to develop sophisticated systems that can provide varying levels of support while consistently respecting resident choice and dignity.

The Human Connection Revolution

The transformation of senior living and post-acute care ultimately depends on the people who provide daily care and support to residents. Comprehensive staff training in emotional intelligence, cultural competency, and relationship-centered care is becoming essential as communities recognize that technical skills alone are insufficient for creating meaningful resident experiences. Staff members are being developed as *relationship builders* who understand that their role extends far beyond task completion to encompass emotional support, genuine companionship, and collaborative problem-solving.

The multicultural and multigenerational nature of today's workforce presents both opportunities and challenges that progressive communities are addressing through innovative training and support systems. These programs help staff members understand and appreciate the diverse backgrounds and experiences of both their colleagues and the residents they serve, creating more inclusive and supportive environments for everyone.

The emphasis on creating meaningful human connections recognizes that technology, while powerful, cannot replace the fundamental human need for genuine relationships that radiate hospitality. Staff members must be equipped with the right knowledge, skills, attitudes, and support necessary to form authentic connections with residents, understanding their individual stories, preferences, and aspirations while providing professional care that honors their dignity and autonomy.

The Future: Caring With, Not For

This transformation from "caring for" to "caring with" represents more than a semantic shift; it embodies a fundamental reimagining of the relationship among senior living and post-acute care providers, their staff, and their customers. This new model positions residents as active partners in their care and community life, recognizing their wisdom, experience, and ongoing capacity for growth and contribution. As these trends continue to evolve, they promise to create environments that not only meet the practical needs of aging but celebrate the ongoing potential and dignity of every employee and resident.

Giving Homework

One of my clients in New Hampshire became a Kind Dining trainer. As the administrator, she would give homework to her staff if they brought her a problem. She wanted them to reframe the conversation and come to her with a solution. The focus then became on problem-solving. And they did a lot of problem-solving to make their hospitality and service better.

This could be something simple: Staff changed whether water glasses were stacked on top of each other down or up. If they were stacked facing down, it was sanitary. That way, when someone grabs the glass, they are grabbing it from the bottom of the glass and not from the top where someone drinks.

They were empowered to be caring rather than to care for. They were trained to know the difference between "service" and "hospitality." And that made a major impact on the lives of the residents and the noble work of the staff.

This is noble work that you are undertaking—make no mistake. Senior care communities need more individuals like you who want to do more and do better.

Thank you for taking on this work and continuing to improve how you do it. You may not notice it, but believe me, your community does.

Appendix

Acknowledgments

God does give second chances, and what you decide to do next is key. After heart failure on October 16, 2019, I never imagined transforming the Kind Dining® curriculum to an online platform and writing a second book, which would honor the ownership transition of the Kind Dining training program to a larger market audience through the amazing guidance of the DiningRD organization.

I am grateful to my family: Husband Mike Heilman, of fifty-one years, the Good Samaritan. Our daughter Katrina Heilman, the inventor of the *Brushi®—Patented Sunscreen Applicator*. Without you, the 6 Truths would not be here. Thank you for your creative design concepts for the front cover. My sister Jody Sullivan, nephew Stephen Thomsen, niece Kayleigh Ross, Mike T. & MaryAnn Maslin. I love you all and thank you for your unending love and continual support.

I am grateful to my extended family members and friends: Brother from another mother, Ken Sandall, and Barbi-Phelps Sandall, our Camino companion, not just once but twice. My False Island family, too many to list, but special mention to John Harmening, Oz Kendall, Jan Donnelly, Joe Parrish, and Lisa Louie—thank you.

Thank you to three professors at Oregon State University who positively influenced my journey towards healthcare: Ann Messersmith, whom I've introduced, and Zoe Anne Holmes and Dr. Leonard Friedman.

Thank you to Marie and Shelley Banfe; you both have been instrumental in your unique talents and skills to keep me forward-thinking, grounded, faithful, and encouraged throughout the difficulties of life and of being a solopreneur.

To Marilyn Sanguinetti and Leah Brandis, for all the hours we spent together with the Making Oregon Vital for Elders movement (M.O.V.E.) and lasting friendship after, thank you for your dedicated energy and support for my speaking, training, and book mission.

I am grateful to the dear friends who have since passed from this earth and have helped drive my mission and vision: Aleta Bauer, Phyllis Mason, and Marla Miller. As I have journeyed onward, I continue to feel the presence of your love, spirit, kind words, and laughter.

I am grateful to my clients, colleagues, and friends who shared their stories for this book: Diana White, Terese Scollard, Vicki Abbate, Audrey Morgan, Janelle Wallace, Sarah McEvoy, and Kathryn Kindopp. Thank you for your trust and friendship.

I am grateful to work colleagues, coaches, and publishers: *To Arlene Bice, thank you for your friendship, writing mentorship*, and for the words you penned and stories you wove to bring my life experiences working in senior living communities to life in our Kind Dining newsletters and readership.

Thank you to Melanie Davis and Mary Tucker, who worked tirelessly behind the scenes to keep our web presence vibrant and informative and our online training platform easy to use and responsive.

Thank you to Patrick McGowan, who enhanced my presence on Zoom as we emerged out of the pandemic.

Thank you to Mark LeBlanc, who has been my one-of-a-kind business coach and who made the difference in my company's success. Thank you for connecting me to Henry DeVries, Indie Books International co-founder and publisher, and his entire creative team.

With a special mention and thank you to my editor, Lisa Apolinski. With your guidance, mastery, wisdom, and humor, you brought out the best in me to write a whole new book, with a new purpose and perspective.

I believe this book will broaden your influence and help you build better relationships with service providers. Proper hospitality training equips caregiving, food service, and ancillary staff teams to shine a light on the dining experience and beyond. I believe it will also provide insight into what matters most for you, dear readers. It will invite you to take this knowledge away and use it in your life, in senior living, and in your post-acute care workplace.

B

Golden Rule Mastery

The Golden Rule is an ancient idea: Do unto others as you would want them to do unto you. I apply this to hospitality in its purist form: to do unto others *first*, which is the quickest way to create a community of belonging.

People always ask me: What is a community of belonging?

It's where the issues of loneliness and isolation experienced by your residents *and* staff are reduced. Kind Dining helps you build that space.

As a leader, you will see two things happen when you implement the Kind Dining Hospitality approach:

- First, you will see an increase in satisfaction and well-being of your residents and families; second, you will see a decrease in staff turnover.
- Why does this work? Because civility and hospitality reward both the giver and receiver.
- And when combined, you get a community of belonging where you see happy and healthy people, which is good for business.

I say "mastery" because it is something that we need to choose to do and practice every single day, at every meal, in every human encounter. My dad taught me about the Golden Rule principle, not just in his words but in his actions. He never met a stranger. My parents (Bill and Evelyn Sullivan) built a strong foundation of love, kindness, faith, and trust. And these were often expressed around mealtimes with family and friends.

But also for this very reason, giving all diligence, add to your faith virtue, to virtue knowledge, to knowledge self-control, to self-control perseverance, to perseverance godliness, to godliness brotherly kindness, to brotherly kindness love.

2 PETER 1: 5-7 (NEW KING JAMES VERSION)

Service Standards

Characteristics Of An Effective Standard:

Clear The reader should get a clear picture of what behavior is expected. Plain language is a must.	**Concise** Keep it Short and Simple (KISS for short). No ambiguous phrases, no vague terminology.
Confirmable Each standard should describe a behavior that can be seen, heard, or measured. An observer should have no trouble determining whether the standard was met or not.	**Challenging** Standards should challenge the service team to excellence, but they can't be so lofty or idealistic they can't be achieved.

Service Statements That Include A Standard:

- Server greets diners within one minute of seating with a warm smile and a friendly greeting.
- Servers know basic ingredients used in recipes for every meal.
- We have a service recovery plan for the five most common problems/complaints. When any of these occur, we follow that plan.
- Food orders are repeated back to the resident to ensure accuracy.
- We have a host/hostess/conductor for every meal every day to ensure the meal flows well.
- Residents who require assistance will not have to wait more than five minutes to receive help leaving the dining room.

The standards and service statements have been adapted from The Vision Standards And Measures Management Module as part of the Kind Dining Training through DiningRD.

About The Author

Cindy Heilman, MS, NDTR, FAND, is a civility builder who transforms aging services communities through the power of exceptional dining experiences. With fifty years focused on dining as it relates to service and hospitality, she has dedicated her career to creating meaningful connections between residents and staff in community living environments.

Cindy holds a master of science degree from Oregon State University with a focus on service priorities in dining for post-acute and senior living communities from the resident's perspective. Cindy has received the Dietetic Technician of the Year Award for the state of Oregon as well as the American Dietetic Association Award for Excellence in Dietetic Technology.

As the creator of Kind Dining, her proprietary training program, Cindy helps staff members understand their vital role in fostering dignity, respect, and genuine caring for one another. She has worked with aging services communities in the US and Canada to reduce loneliness and isolation by building better relationships around the dining table and beyond it. She continues this noble work as part of DiningRD. Her mission is to promote hospitality, civility, and love within the communities that aging adults call home.

She resides in the greater Portland area with her husband, Mike. In her free time, she enjoys walking Oregon trails, cheering on her favorite local women's soccer team, the Portland Thorns, and growing dahlias, her latest hobby.

A little-known fact about Cindy: She has ocean kayaked throughout Southeast Alaska, often camping and cooking among its many Alaskan brown bears.

E

Works Cited

1 Quint Studer and Dan Collard, "Rewiring Leadership In Post-acute Healthcare: Equipping Leaders To Succeed," accessed November 12, 2025, https://healthcareplussg.com/book/rewiring-leadership-in-post-acute-healthcare/.

2 Chrissy Daniels, "Patient experience in 2024: Bridging the gap in patient care journeys," PressGaney, August 20, 2024, https://info.pressganey.com/press-ganey-blog-healthcare-experience-insights/patient-experience-in-2024-bridging-the-gap.

3 "Social eating connects communities," University of Oxford, March 17, 2017, https://www.ox.ac.uk/news/2017-03-16-social-eating-connects-communities.

4 Bob Kramer, "Hospitality's Immense Opportunity in the New Senior Living," Boston University School of Hospitality Administration, May 24, 2022, https://www.bu.edu/bhr/2022/05/24/hospitalitys-opportunity-senior-living/.

5 "well-being." 2026a. In M*erriam-Webster Dictionary*. https://www.merriam-webster.com/dictionary/well-being.

6 Amy Bollam, "Six Truths for Success You Cannot Ignore," DiningRD, April 19, 2024, https://www.diningrd.com/blog/six-truths-for-success-you-cannot-ignore/.

7 "Research Priorities," Nutrition & Foodservice Education Foundation, accessed November 12, 2025, https://www.anfponline.org/foundation/research#.

8 "Social eating connects communities."

9 "Minnesota Assisted Living and Nursing Home Quality of Life Surveys," Vital Research, accessed November 12, 2025, https://vitalresearch.com/mnsurvey/facility/ALOverview.html.

10 Susanna Guzman, "How Much Does Independent Living Cost? A State-by-State Guide," A Place For Mom, March 21, 2025, https://www.aplaceformom.com/caregiver-resources/articles/independent-senior-living-costs.

11 "Person-Centered Care," Centers for Medicare and Medicaid, https://www.cms.gov/priorities/innovation/key-concepts/person-centered-care.

12 Quint Studer, *The Calling: Why Healthcare Is So Special* (The Gratitude Group Publishing, 2022).

13 Gretchen M. Spreitzer and Christine Porath, "Creating Sustainable Performance," *Harvard Business Review*, January-February 2012, https://hbr.org/2012/01/creating-sustainable-performance.

14 Deidre H. Campbell, "What Great Companies Know About Culture," *Harvard Business Review*, December 14, 2011, https://hbr.org/2011/12/what-great-companies-know-about.

15 Elois Ann Berlin and William C. Fowkes Jr., "A Teaching Framework for Cross-cultural Health Care—Application in Family Practice," *Western Journal of Medicine*, December 1983, 139(6): 934–938, https://pmc.ncbi.nlm.nih.gov/articles/PMC1011028/.

16 Rosamund Stone Zander and Benjamin Zander, *The Art of Possibility: Transforming Professional and Personal Life* (Penguin Books, 2002).

17 Diana Whiteet al., "Supporting Nursing Home Staff Through Person-Centered Care Practices," *Innovation in Aging* 3, no. Supplement_1 (November 1, 2019): S698–99, https://doi.org/10.1093/geroni/igz038.2571.

18 Diana White and Serena Hasworth, "'They Don't Have Time, but It Would Be Wonderful': Residents' Views of Their Relationships With Staff," *Journal of Gerontological Nursing* 49, no. 11 (October 31, 2023): 8–14, https://doi.org/10.3928/00989134-20231010-03.

19 White and Hasworth, "'They Don't Have Time, but It Would Be Wonderful': Residents' Views of Their Relationships With Staff."

20 Will Guidara, *Unreasonable Hospitality: The Remarkable Power of Giving People More Than They Expect* (Optimum Press, 2022).

21 Steve Shields, *In Pursuit of the Sunbeam: A Practical Guide to Transformation from Institution to Household* (Action Pact Press, 2006).

22 White et al., "Supporting Nursing Home Staff Through Person-Centered Care Practices."

23 Robert L. Scharff, "State Estimates for the Annual Cost of Foodborne Illness," *Journal of Food Protection* 78, no. 6 (June 1, 2015): 1064–71, https://doi.org/10.4315/0362-028x.jfp-14-505.

24 Jack Cumming, "Dining at Home," *Senior Living Foresight*, June 23, 2025, https://www.seniorlivingforesight.net/dining-at-home/.

25 "Understanding Assisted Living Cost: Key Factors and Variations," SeniorSite, accessed November 19, 2025, https://seniorsite.org/resource/understanding-assisted-living-cost-key-factors-and-variations/.

26 Amy Stulick, "Slash Food Spending Below $10 a Day," *Skilled Nursing News*, April 30, 2025, https://skillednursingnews.com/2025/04/more-than-25-of-nursing-homes-slash-food-spending-below-10-a-day/#.

27 "Bridging the Gap: Dining Leaders Shape the Resident Experience," *Senior Dining*, July 21, 2025, https://seniordining.org/senior-dining-news/f/bridging-the-gap-dining-leaders-shape-the-resident-experience.

28 Quint Studer and Dr. Anthony Stanowski, "How Team Leaders Foster Skill Development in Others: Quint Studer on Leaders as Teachers," Master Your Healthcare Career (video), Season 2, Episode 3, October 3, 2023, https://www.buzzsprout.com/1808131/episodes/13708590-how-team-leaders-foster-skill-development-in-others-quint-studer-on-leaders-as-teachers.

29 Frederic Chopin, https://www.azquotes.com/quote/869528.

30 Preeti Malani, MD, MS, MSJ; Jeff Kullgren, MD, MPH, MS; Scott Roberts, PhD, MA, "Loneliness and isolation: Back to pre-pandemic levels, but still high, for older adults," University of Michigan Institute for Healthcare Policy & Innovation, December 9, 2024, https://ihpi.umich.edu/news-events/news/loneliness-and-isolation-back-pre-pandemic-levels-still-high-older-adults.

31 Joyce Simard and Ladislav Volicer, "Loneliness and Isolation in Long-term Care and the COVID-19 Pandemic," *Journal of the American Medical Directors Association*, May 8, 2020; 21(7):966–967, https://pmc.ncbi.nlm.nih.gov/articles/PMC7205644/.

32 "Unlocking Staffing Success in Senior Living: Retention Strategies That Work," LCS Living, July 7, 2023, https://www.lcsliving.com/resources/for-providers/senior-living-development/unlocking-staffing-success-in-senior-living-retention-strategies-that-work/.

33 Guidara, *Unreasonable Hospitality: The Remarkable Power of Giving People More Than They Expect*, 7.

34 Austin Montgomery, "How Senior Living Operators Are Turning the Page on Turnover," *Senior Housing News*, November 30, 2023, https://seniorhousingnews.com/2023/11/30/how-senior-living-operators-are-turning-the-page-on-turnover/.

35 "The ROI of quality care in senior living facilities," ProviderCAS, January 4, 2024, https://providercas.com/the-roi-of-quality-care-in-senior-living-facilities/.

36 Cindy Heilman, *Hospitality for Boomers: How to attract residents, retain staff, and maximize profitability* (Cindy Heilman Self Publishing, 2012).

37 Cara Silletto, MBA, CSP, "Today's Workforce Isn't What It Used to Be—And That's Not a Bad Thing," LinkedIn, August 18, 2025, https://www.linkedin.com/pulse/todays-workforce-isnt-what-used-beand-thats-bad-thing-cara-z2e3f/.

38 Christine Porath and Christine Pearson, "The Price of Uncivility," *Harvard Butiness Review*, Jan-Feb 2013, https://www.qualitymanagementinstitute.com/images/hrsolutions/HBR-ThePriceofIncivility.pdf.

Index

www.ingramcontent.com/pod-product-compliance
Lightning Source LLC
Chambersburg PA
CBHW030235160926
51579CB00030B/168
9781966168744